eYE MARTY

MY LIFE IN WORDS AND PICTURES

Marty Feldman

CORONET

First published in Great Britain in 2015 by Coronet
An imprint of Hodder & Stoughton
An Hachette UK company

First published in paperback in 2016

1

Copyright © Marty Feldman/Mark Flanagan 2015

The right of Marty Feldman to be identified as the Author of the Work has been
asserted by him in accordance with the Copyright, Designs and Patents Act 1988.

A CIP catalogue record for this title is available from the British Library

Paperback ISBN: 978 1 444 79273 7
Ebook ISBN: 978 1 444 79276 8

Typeset in Sabon by Hewer Text UK Ltd, Edinburgh

Printed and bound by Clays Ltd, St Ives

Hodder & Stoughton policy is to use papers that are natural, renewable
and recyclable products and made from wood grown in sustainable
forests. The logging and manufacturing processes are expected to
conform to the environmental regulations of the country of origin.

Hodder & Stoughton Ltd
Carmelite House
50 Victoria Embankment
London EC4Y 0DZ

www.hodder.co.uk

B|FEL

Marty Feldman was a comedy writer, comedian and actor. Feldman was born in the East End of London in 1934. By the age of 20 he had decided to pursue a career as a comedian.

The sketch comedy series *At Last the 1948 Show* featured Feldman's first screen performances. The other three performers – future Pythons Graham Chapman and John Cleese, and future Goodie Tim Brooke-Taylor needed a fourth and had Feldman in mind. Marty was co-author the famous Monty Python 'Four Yorkshiremen' sketch and was also script editor on *The Frost Report* with future members of Monty Python.

In 1968 Marty was given his own series by the BBC called *Marty*, it featured Brooke-Taylor, John Junkin and Roland MacLeod with John Cleese as one of the writers. Feldman won two BAFTA awards. The *Marty* series proved popular enough with an international audience to launch a film career. His first feature role was in *Every Home Should Have One*.

Marty Feldman was married to Lauretta Sullivan from January 1959 until his death in 1982. Feldman died from a heart attack in December 1982 at the age of 48. He is buried in the Hollywood Hills Cemetary near his idol, Buster Keaton.

THE CLOWN PRINCE

ERIC IDLE

Marty was on my first honeymoon. That's bizarre, isn't it? But I recommend having a comedian on honeymoon as it gives you something to do in the daytime. Especially somebody as funny as Marty. We lay by the sea in the South of France and laughed and laughed and laughed. That was July 1969 and *Monty Python* was just beginning, due in no small part to him.

For a long time the two of us had talked about mounting a comedy tour of Australia, and though we spent that snowy Christmas in Marty and Lauretta's house in Hampstead, drinking and laughing the nights away, our lives were to go in different directions as he rocketed to international fame and we began the obscure late-night TV show we expected no one to see.

I had first met Marty three years earlier, in 1966, when I was a new and very young writer on *The Frost Report*. He was exceptionally kind and supportive to all of us – Michael Palin, Terry Jones, John Cleese, Graham Chapman and Tim Brooke-Taylor, young writers scooped up into the world of David Frost – and we soon became pals, sharing a love of white wine, jazz, Italian food, flared pants and football. We played 'soccer' together on Sundays in Hyde Park and occasionally in charity matches. I remember one such at Ford Open Prison: after it was in the papers that Marty had been burgled and lost lots of clothes, the inmates solemnly presented him with a prison suit. He was very touched. That day, on the way home, we stopped at a random Italian restaurant in the middle of nowhere and Marty talked the owner into turning on the telly. There, on a flickering set, we watched the first live pictures of the moon landing.

Back in the early days when we first met, Marty was 'only' a writer, but what a writer! He would take us to the recordings of the extremely naughty and sublimely successful *Round the Horne*: we would howl at the cleverness of his and Barry Took's writing for Kenneth Williams and Hugh Paddick, as they camped about speaking Palare, the gay lingo Marty himself spoke all the time with Lauretta.

'Oo varda the lallies on that omey!' he'd shriek. 'Varda the eek!' ('Oo, look at the legs on that man! And look at that face') followed by Lauretta's frequently used warning, 'Schtum, nante the palare, fingers earwigging.' ('Shush, keep quiet, there's somebody listening.')

In 1966 Marty was an unknown face to the public, but what a face. Mischievous, ironic, iconic, he used his quizzical physiognomy to his advantage, playing tricks publicly on all of us. 'No, I will not come back to your place, you filthy man,' he yelled at a packed Chelsea ground, striding away from a blushing Tim Brooke-Taylor. I saw him play the same gag on John Cleese on a Tube escalator. He loved crowds and felt completely safe in them, and his looks gave him the excuse to behave outrageously long before he was famous for them. In a crowded London restaurant he would taste the proffered wine, savour it, roll it around in his mouth, then suddenly clutch his throat, howl and throw himself to the floor, to the consternation of the waiter and the other diners. Then he'd pick himself up, sit down, nod at the waiter and say, 'Yes, that's fine.' Sadly, after he became famous, he could no longer play these tricks – his face had outed him as a comedian – but right from the first he dressed and behaved extravagantly and was utterly generous with his time and money. 'All you need is love, luv,' he said to me once, declining cash, when I hit him up for a lump of hash.

I think he liked us Oxbridge crowd because he could see he had missed nothing in not going to college, and we loved him for his advice, helping us navigate the strange world of showbiz we were all entering. It was the age of the Beatles, it was the age of the Stones, and there was a new world happening out there.

In 1967 John Cleese was putting together a TV show called *At Last the 1948 Show*, and insisted that Marty be in it, against the express doubts of the producer, David Frost, who was worried that Marty's looks would scare the audience. Fortunately John got his way and the rest is history: a star was born, and within a couple of years he had become the biggest TV star in the UK with *Marty*.

After an extremely fast rise to the top, Marty went into the movies and eventually to Hollywood where, thanks to Gene Wilder, he joined the circus of the amazing Mel Brooks. He had tremendous success there, followed, inevitably in showbiz, by some failures. In Hollywood failure is seen as a contagious disease – and there is a legendary story that after a second film flopped he threw a party and nobody came. I can't really believe that. He can't have invited anybody real, because no one sensible would ever have opted out of his company. When we, by now famous, Pythons arrived to play the Hollywood Bowl in 1980 there were parties galore for us with Steve Martin, Martin Scorsese, Harry Nilsson, Ringo Starr and George. Marty relished our success and was proud of us. There was no envy or jealousy. It was as if we were younger family members who had made it too.

Flash forward to autumn 1982 and Marty came into our kitchen in Carlton Hill, London. He was thin as a wraith and pale, chain-smoking, talking non-stop, but grinning as always and thrilled to be back in the UK to work with Graham Chapman, Peter Cook, John and me on *Yellowbeard*. It really felt like a homecoming to him, to be back in England to make a dumb film about pirates with all his old pals. The best thing was that after two weeks in Rye, Sussex, we got to go on location in Mexico, and what a great trip that was. Peter Cook was sober and in the best form of his life, and there were hilarious people, like Peter Boyle, Kenneth Mars, Madeline Kahn and Cheech and Chong, to play with. Marty appeared healthier and was having a blast busily stealing the picture. He is certainly the funniest thing in it.

After a few weeks by the sea we all moved to Mexico City, where I finished my work on the film in early November and went off to Australia. It was a month later, while I was in Sydney, that I heard Marty had died.

He would have hated being portrayed as the sad clown. He was a very happy clown: indeed, the clown prince. He lived a very full life doing what he loved doing, making people laugh, with the love of his life beside him, except, tragically, at the end. It was an absence for which Lauretta never forgave herself, although there was nothing she could possibly have done to prevent it. Mexican traffic is notoriously awful and the ambulance could not get through to save him from the heart attack he would most likely have survived in LA. He was only forty-eight.

> *Life's a piece of shit*
> *When you look at it.*

This autobiography, mercifully rescued from an attic by the generous and thoughtful 'Flanny' Flanagan, reveals the writer that Marty was, warts and all. Funny, provocative, occasionally ridiculous, there is no attempt here to settle old scores or wound others or justify himself. He was a compassionate man who loved people. I'm really thrilled that he can finally tell, in his own words, the strange and hilarious world that he illuminated with his kindness and his gifts.

I just went to the web to ask how many people remembered him and loved him after thirty years. I was inundated with thousands of replies, a real outpouring of love and affection. 'Genius'; 'Loved him'; 'Can we ever forget?'; 'One of the funniest men to walk the earth' . . . I was swamped by all the responses and thrilled to see there is no possibility that my friend will soon be forgotten.

Say no more.

Eric Idle, January 2013

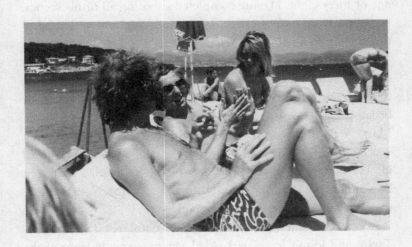

EDITOR'S NOTE
MARK FLANAGAN

Lauretta Eleanor Sullivan knew from the moment she met Martin Alan Feldman that he would be the love of her life and that they would spend the rest of their lives together till death did they part. She described her husband Marty as her 'old man'. He was her soulmate and best friend, and the funniest, smartest, sexiest person she had ever met.

Marty died on location for a film on 2 December 1982, at the age of forty-eight. Having completed shooting all of his scenes, he was staying an extra day or two in case they needed additional shots. The film was *Yellowbeard*.

His good friend Graham Chapman had talked him into doing the film even though he knew that Marty was desperately trying to get back into a career as a writer. Marty wasn't sure but because Graham was asking he agreed: he felt he owed him. Marty was an actor and director and loved both, but writing was his true passion and a profession he felt he had more control in. He had been a very successful and influential writer in England before shooting into stardom as an actor. Now his creative writing juices were flowing again.

It was Graham who, with his then flatmates Tim Brooke-Taylor and John Cleese, persuaded Marty to step in front of the camera in *At Last the 1948 Show*, and Marty always felt indebted to his friends for this, much to the chagrin of the show's producer: David Frost was convinced that Marty's looks were too grotesque and that the public would be turned off by his strange eyEs.

That, of course, was not the case and Marty became an overnight sensation in Britain.

The film was not just going to be a good paying gig but was to feature many of Marty's friends, including Graham, John Cleese, Eric Idle, Peter Cook, Madeline Kahn, Peter Boyle, David Bowie, Marty's pal Harry Nilsson, and his hero and friend Spike Milligan. It would be a working holiday for him and Lauretta.

From the moment of their first meeting until the day he died, Lauretta and Marty had rarely been apart for more than a few days, mostly when Lauretta went home early to get the house in shape for his return.

The day Marty shot his final scene, Graham received a frantic call from him: 'Please come quickly – I think I'm dying.'

Graham, who was not just a great friend but also a trained doctor, rushed to Marty's room, knowing from the tone of his voice that this was not a prank. The door was locked and he needed help to force it open. Marty was still alive but labouring, and Graham asked someone to call an ambulance and retrieve the hotel's emergency equipment. It was not enough to save him. The ambulance arrived long after he had died and the oxygen tank was empty. Peter Cook pleaded with all who witnessed Marty's passing that it must remain a secret until someone could tell Lauretta, who was at home waiting for her husband to return.

John Cleese, who was co-starring in the film and had been a great friend to them both, tried in vain to reach her. He also contacted mutual friends in LA and asked them to find her.

Marty was being treated for a severe back problem and had told Lauretta that it was worsening. She had set up an appointment for him to see a specialist when he got home. She was very worried. They spoke on the phone every day, often several times.

On the day of his death she went shopping, and planned an early dinner with friends, as she had told Marty on the phone. Otherwise no one knew where she was. Eventually someone contacted her close friends Stanley Schneider, Georgia Brown and Stanley Dorfman, among others.

When Lauretta arrived home and saw cars in her drive, she had no idea what was going on. Maybe her housekeeper was throwing a party. She had passed many houses on her way home with Christmas decorations on display and wondered if it had something to do with that.

She went in through the back door, as she always did, to find her friends gathered in the kitchen. She was delighted but confused. Then she experienced a sudden chill, which ran through her entire body. Stanley tried to tell her what had happened, but failed. Finally Georgia held her face with both hands, looked her in the eyes and said, 'Lauretta, Marty is gone.'

I met Lauretta ten years after Marty had died, and we became friends.

When she first told me the story of his death she expressed anger towards the director and producers for pushing Marty too hard, when they knew he was suffering from a severe medical condition. She also knew, and would say, that Marty was a maniac and always insisted on doing his own stunts, no matter what, much to the horror of his directors, who pleaded with her over the years to make him stop. Mel Brooks drove her crazy, insisting that she talk Marty out of it.

Lauretta frequently talked about Marty's writing and thought it was sad that, after his death, no one would care any more about that aspect of his career. She told me that all of his writings were safely stored in the attic and joked, 'There's gold in them there hills.' She never wanted to see or read them after he had gone because she would find it too difficult. Photographs were less of a challenge: the house was full of them.

She knew he had been working for years on an autobiography and remembered him writing with more urgency in the six months leading up to his death. He would constantly run into the kitchen to ask her for somebody's name or if such-and-such had happened before or after something else.

On 10 March 2010 Lauretta passed away at home after a short battle with brain cancer. She looked as beautiful as always and was clasping a poem that Marty had written for her, with birds chirping in her garden.

A month or so beforehand I had moved into her house to keep her company and help her. We both knew the end was near. She became very concerned that all of Marty's boxes were safe and, thankfully, they were. She felt his story should be published somewhere – maybe I could put it on the internet? Many articles and documentaries had come and gone, but Lauretta hadn't liked any of them: she said they always tried to peg Marty as another clichéd sad clown.

She had been asked several times to write her own autobiography, but had always felt the publishers were after his story, not hers. She might have been wrong. Years before, when my mother died, Lauretta told me that I would get past it but never over it, and that she would be with me always.

She was right. It took me a long while to get past Lauretta's death. A year after she had gone, I started going through the boxes she had kept in her attic. One was marked 'eyE Marty'. Inside, I found Marty's small typewriter, plus clippings and photographs, with meticulous notes, such as 'insert Lauretta on bike photo' or 'include Sperm poem'. They were attached to a script with 'eyE Marty' on the first page. It was Marty's autobiography, his story, with all its twists and turns. None of his writing has been changed and all of his attachments have been included. The photographs on the front and back covers of the book were Lauretta's favourites, and were taken a few days before his death. He looks vibrant, full of life and mischief.

His life was short but it packed a punch. Above all, his love for his old lady prevails throughout.

For Lauretta and Marty

GOODBYE

I remember holdin' on to you
All them long lonely nights I put you through
Somewhere in there I'm sure I made you cry
But I can't remember if we said
Goodbye
But I recall all of them nights down in Mexico
One place I may never go in my life again
Was I off somewhere or just too high
But I can't remember if we said goodbye
I only miss you every now and then
Like the soft breeze blowin' up from the Caribbean
Most Novembers I break down and cry
'cause I can't remember if we said goodbye

Steve Earle

NOTE FROM THE AUTHOR

Everything that one writes must be a result of what has happened to these nine holes. That being said, recently I did an audit of my personal books and I now know I have certain limitations. I will never play football for Chelsea, and I won't ever be a tight-rope walker. These are things that I can't do physically because of my age, my parents, that sort of thing. My face reflects the disasters of my life so far. My eyEs are the by-product of a thyroid condition, perhaps brought on by an accident when a boy stuck a pencil in my eyE at school or the result of a boating mishap, when I almost drowned, that left one eyE rather lazy. My nose was broken and bent by not catching cricket balls or by poorly arranged fights, and my height is slight at best.

My looks are my comic equipment, and they are the right packaging for my job. Not the right packaging for a brain surgeon or the pilot of a 747, but I have the right packaging for a clown.

I need comedy and there's nothing degrading about playing the fool. When the looks fade I will still have the writing to fall back on!

Extreme youth and old age have much in common. At both ends of life there is a sense of diminished responsibility: neither the very young nor the very old are involved with the business of day-to-day living. The young have not reached the point where the affairs of the world and the struggle to succeed in life are their concern, and the old are beyond the battle. Here, then, a brief excursion down Memory Lane, with side trips into cul-de-sacs.

But first! Why me and poor you? I've been picking away at this life story of mine on and mostly off for years. I should give all credit to my wife and other half, Lauretta, whose screams of 'Write, Mart! It's what you do!' echo around our house whenever she hears me rant about not working or when she sees me staring at the wall like a loon.

I first had the idea of a collection of short stories, some autobiographical and others fictional with fun photos and stuff. It morphed into my life story, or body map, if you will, and this is my third draft.

I have luckily kept busy working and living, so this exercise of thinking about myself, all that I have done and been through, hasn't completely consumed me and turned me into a monster.

I am just a being with monster parts.

I've grown to think of myself as a writer first and everything else afterwards, but the truth is I have only ever written well with other people. So, I set myself this task, this autobiographical rant, with my career-self as co-pilot.

I left school way too young and could never be described as educated. Having said that, I have read and continue to read every book I can get my hands on. My career success could easily be credited to what I have read about other performers. My shelves are filled with books. Most are biographies with no particular genre – sports people, entertainers, all inspiring because of the obstacles they have overcome. So, the hope is that someone will find something in here to move them along on their path, like Buster Keaton, Miles Davis and so many others have with me. Narcissism is defined as self-infatuation. In my case it is not infatuation but the real thing!

It's just as lonely at the bottom as it is at the top, but it is terribly crowded in the middle, so I am ruthlessly clawing my way to the bottom.

Now done with looking backwards – or, with my eyEs, kind of backwards but also a bit to the side – I have come to terms with certain facts as I edge into the age Wayne Shorter refers to as intermediate-elderly.

I have made it my primary task to be dedicated and determined to translate the complete speeches of Ronald Reagan into English.

For Lauretta: You are a seasoned woman, a woman not perhaps for all seasons, for your season is spring. Happy Wednesday, I do love you.

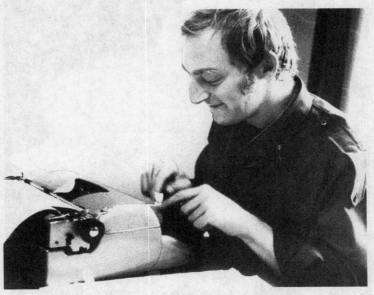

The pen is mightier than the sword and considerably
easier to write with!

How honest can you get?

SPERM

Just like you, just like me
We began as a little drop of sperm
So don't forget where you came from
And here's a thought to make you squirm
So no matter who you are
Just remember where you were
You began as a little drop of sperm
Einstein, Muhammad Ali, you and me

BEGIN

My head is like a dusty attic full of everything I ever thought, tasted, felt, smelt, lived and loved. It's all stuffed up there.

When I write, I go wandering around this attic, stumbling over things, banging my shins on ideas, and I don't always know where to find them. Some writers have minds like filing cabinets; mine is not.

How far back can nostalgia go? Nostalgia isn't what it was and the great thing about the future is that it can't catch up on you. By the time I finish saying this . . .

I was born and named Martin Alan Feldman on 8 July 1934, at University College Hospital, London. I was discharged a day later, only to find that my university and college days were now behind me and never to return.

At one time I wanted to be a pilot. In fact, I told my parents that I was a pilot at only four years of age. I also told them that I was not their son: I was Bing Crosby's brother, and had been dropped into England as a spy. I thought Bing was going to come and reclaim me.

I was never going to be an actor or a comedian because I didn't think those were things people became. I thought comedians in particular were always here, born like that. Perhaps because I really was a pretty boy who became an odd-looking teenager and an odder-looking adult, I was born later.

If only we could redesign ourselves for the function we need. Maybe all we need is a top and a pair of legs to carry it around and an eyE set in it. So, I am constantly told, the body is a marvellous machine. That may be so, but it is in fact a lousy package – the almighty architect could easily have been outdone by a second-year art student in designing a more functional human being. Let's rethink the whole thing from the beginning, like Darwin. Very simply, our nose is in the wrong place. Anybody who realises that the main function of the nose is to smell what you eat would place the nose where it would not get in the way of the mouth. I would put my cock at the end of my finger. It would make shaking hands a lot more fun. Even pointing out a direction would be more interesting. Think of a crowded train station with a cock on your shoulder. Very friendly indeed! I do think the cock is in the wrong place. It is badly placed for the way we stand. We stand on two legs, and in order to use our cocks more effectively we have to sort of crouch in an undignified position, but if we had it on our finger it would be quite useful: we could spear things with it. The eyEs, too, are in the wrong place. I am probably more aware of this than most because I have an eyE that looks the opposite way from the other.

But why should we not have an eyE that can see all around us? Well, we are what we are but we could be so much more.

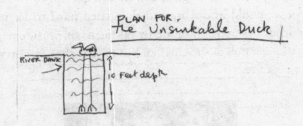

PLAN FOR:
The Unsinkable Duck

RIVER BANK → 10 Feet depth

My earliest memory is probably of Laurel and Hardy in a film, which I saw when I was about five. I think it was at the Granada Cinema in Canning Town. I remember that film very well – I saw it again recently on telly and it was exactly as I remembered it.

The East End of London and Canning Town had not changed in hundreds of years. They built the first council houses there in an attempt to provide better homes for the area's inhabitants. Charles Dickens described it better than most so go and get his books after you have enjoyed mine. Some people who were born into an impoverished environment are able to look back fondly and say they didn't know they were impoverished because of the love of their family and friends. I had that love aplenty and still look back in horror at the conditions my parents had to cope with.

Canning Town was reeling from the First World War and another war was on the way. The area didn't need those events to make life grim: it was just more hardship for people who were living in rubble already. It was always dark and damp. It was docklands, and we always felt submerged.

Most of the people who lived there were of immigrant stock and, as in most slums worldwide, lived in the shadow of wealthy neighbours. There was a sense of community but there was also anger, resentment and danger at every turn. I really admire my

23

parents for pulling through it all. We did get out of the area as soon as we could afford it, and they tried hard to let us have some sort of normal childhood by taking us on seaside trips and letting us see a film at the cinema. But mostly they were trying to save and escape.

Cinema for me, and most kids, offered a temporary escape. Laurel and Hardy had a tremendous influence on my childhood, as did music, jazz in particular. I was conscious of and collected jazz records at a very early age. At four or five I knew who Benny Goodman and Gene Krupa were. Couldn't get enough of them. I can't think of any good reason why at that age I was so into jazz music. It was the late thirties and it was all around me. Friends and cousins would scrape the pennies together and we would beg, borrow or more often steal to get our hands on records. My uncle was the only one in the area who had a record player: he had stolen it after being fired from Woolworths. We would gather on Sundays and blast our latest finds.

My father came from a family of twelve kids, ten of whom were boys, and all played instruments. I wanted to be a musician but again I thought that this was something you were especially born to be, a prodigy type of thing, which nobody chose to call me so therefore I wasn't one. The trouble is that, all these years later, I still think this way.

I thought if I were to pick up an alto sax that, within an hour or so, I would be able to play like Charlie Parker, so I will never pick one up, and thus will always have potential. This thing inhibits me from walking on a tightrope: as long as I never do it I might be the best in the world.

I have never thought about falling or how I am going to land until I see the ground rising up to meet me. As a result of this, I have had broken arms, concussion and worse from doing stunts, all because I did not think about them in advance.

When I was young I never had a plan for anything except getting out of school or trying to acquire more records to listen to. I do envy people who can work out a plan for life and stick to it until they are sixty-five. They believe every move is planned by a higher power and that they always intended to be where they are in life. Not this klutz.

I am not in any sense an intellectual. I am intuitive or instinctive or both. I do not believe in pure animal intuition – I think we have lost all of that – but I am still liable to think that if you were to offer me one of two choices I would make one without wondering why, then twenty minutes later question whether it was a good choice, and ask myself why I made it.

Everything I have done has been a result of what seem to be rather random acts and I have learned to capitalise on them. I have learned to be quick when I have landed and just as quick to see where I have landed. A moving target is harder to hit.

I was a small kid and didn't grow quickly, then stop, like most kids do. I have always been relatively small. I was a fast runner because I was no good at fighting. Big people are usually not fast runners because they do not need to be: they are rarely picked on or challenged. They can go fast but not too far. It's the little buggers who are the fast ones and often have to run great distances to escape. As a kid I used to run alongside my mates when they were walking down the street. This appears to have conditioned my approach to life. I still tend to trail people when walking and never seem to catch up. I was a Jewish kid in places where most people were not.

They thought a bar mitzvah was a pub my dad worked in. I became the exotic-looking person who would try to keep up with the rest.

I went to eleven or twelve schools. We shifted from Canning Town to Forest Gate, on to Highbury, then to Holly Road. By the time the war came I had been slung out of three schools and run away from another two. I now realise that the standard of schooling for kids is a lot higher than we were up against. And I mean 'up against' because we seemed to be up against it all. Because of the war, we ended up with all the reject teachers. Either they were too old, and should have retired, or they were not fit enough to make the forces. I only ever had one good teacher in all my schooling and this was at boarding school. He was a bloke called Atkinson, who had been a pilot and had been invalided out of the RAF. He was also a painter, which later influenced me. He was in ENSA – Entertainments National Service Association – as a comic, and he used to put on school shows, very strange shows with eleven-year-olds doing mature musical shtick. I somehow responded to all of this. He was also a big football fan, so all my interests come from him because he encouraged me. I owe a lot to the guy. I hope all kids have a figure like him in their lives, who stimulates their interests, usually a parent. My father was in the army at the time so I had my English teacher. I have tried to find him over the years but my efforts have yielded nothing.

I once got 98 per cent in English and 0 per cent in maths in exactly the same set of examinations. I set the record both ways! We used to get five marks for just putting our name at the top of the paper. I put 'Can't Do It' on my maths paper and gave it in. I was a terrible source of embarrassment to the school because I was great at English and bloody awful at maths. They didn't like that. They wanted 50 per cent in everything, which they had set in stone as the norm, whether they were aware of it or not. I think teachers are not as cynical as the society that produces them. They would rather have an average society that talks about averages. That way they can run elections, sell us tooth-paste and manipulate us.

I don't think soldiers are people who have been encouraged to be individuals. Unlike armies, individuals do not have a common cause. I myself have never taken a straight line and would rather go what seems to be the prettiest route. I never made it into the army. I was rejected after my physical examination. I was graded A1 but passed on to a psychiatrist, who graded me A4 because I responded badly to discipline. He thought I would be a bad influence on the other soldiers, which was true.

That is why I made my way towards a life in comedy, because the public encourages anarchy, thereby urging the comic to revolt.

Comics have a valuable function, but perhaps not as valuable as most comics seem to think. There has been a lot of bullshit talked and written about comics, that we can laugh off things that threaten us, which, of course, we cannot. We cannot laugh off war. We can take some of the menace out of it, keep it at a distance, like when we were kids hiding behind the curtains, challenging the bogeyman to come and get us. We can only hide for so long and he will still be there when we come out. If we identify the source of our fear we are less inclined to be afraid. It doesn't mean that it will no longer kill us or destroy us but we won't be afraid of it any more. I have always been aware of what I was doing, then and more so now. Kids can distinguish reality from fantasy, but this ability is diminished as soon as they go to school. I used to get into trouble at school for simply asking, 'Why?' or saying, 'Please explain that to me.' I really wasn't the rebel that I later became: I wanted to learn and fit in. Adam and Eve would be rammed home to us as the truth while something equally fantastic, like 'Three Blind Mice', would be rammed home as fantasy. Do people really believe God made woman out of Adam's rib? 'Three Blind Mice' seems way more real to me. I can imagine what a mouse looks like. I can imagine him chopping off his tail. But a rib turning into a woman? Do me a favour! As a kid I enjoyed *Tom and Jerry*. I knew they'd be squashed and still come back in the next frame. That is reality.

I was always convinced the teachers were after me at school – and they were. That was why I ran away so much. I knew they were trying to knock the kid out of me and I wasn't having it. Most of them spotted the glint of mischief in my eyE and were hell bent on keeping it as a glint. If a kid feels they're being persecuted there is usually a good reason for it. After a while of being persecuted as a kid, you start to think you may as well be a villain because the odds are you're going to get whacked anyway. So I became a villain and got respect mostly for being a jester and troublemaker.

Being Jewish had an extra impact: most of the time I was at schools I had been evacuated to during the war where there weren't as many Jews. So, as well as being a jester, I was regarded as somewhat exotic-looking, long before my eyE and broken nose took exotic to the utmost. I was not considered to be different, more an alien.

Outside my English class, I rarely learned anything I needed. I still think they should teach kids how to survive with what you have. I have never needed Latin: I needed to be taught how to fiddle with my taxes. And maybe instead of track and field we should've been taught how to catch and kill. Equip us to survive as an adult in the twentieth century.

We were discouraged from playing Cowboys and Indians. We should've been taught how to rob and cheat and, most importantly, the art of lying. Those were the coping skills we needed, not proper grammar and bloody trigonometry. Some of the best painters had little formal education, which seems to have benefited their originality. They could barely write their names but produced the most beautiful art we will ever see. Pop music is very much an art-school manifestation, its students, like John Lennon, producing revitalised music.

I didn't do Bible class because I was a Jew, the only Jew in my class. They didn't know what to do with me so gave me extra maths. The Bible must have been hard work because God knows maths was. I used to get annoyed by it and would draw graffiti over the other boys' Bibles when they weren't looking. Once I was sent home for drawing glasses and a moustache on some saint.

I could never resist a dare, which is probably why I do stunts now – I dare myself to do things. I was appointed to ring the bell in the classroom when the master came through the door, calling for order and attention. One day I rang it for too long and he knew I was being sarcastic. He said, 'I dare you to try that outside the headmaster's door.' I, of course, knew this was something I needed to do.

I took the same bell after class, stood outside the headmaster's door and rang it as hard as I could, knowing that all the teachers and students would run out into the yard and I would get whacked. That was exactly what happened.

Even though I know something is going to be a disaster I commit to it. I ought to be declared a disaster area. They certainly thought I was at every school I ever attended.

The third time I ran away from school the head got the hint and asked my parents not to bring me back. To run away from a heated classroom in the cold winter damp of wartime London sounds insane but that was how bad it was.

My parents were more understanding than any other Jewish parents in their social group. Other parents assumed that teachers were right, that they were taking good care of their children's health and education while at school, but in fact they were a bunch of thugs, who went out of their way to beat us or make us feel insignificant.

One of our teachers kicked a girl down a flight of stairs for singing. This made a major impression on me, and still does, even after all these years. The school spun some story about the girl being out of control, and even as she lay in the hospital, broken and fractured, her parents never doubted the teacher's word. Several years later the school was closed down. My parents at least acknowledged I was having a rough go of it and tried moving me around, hoping that their square peg would eventually find its proper hole. The trouble with being an anarchist is that you end up blowing up the building you live in.

I have Russian-Polish ancestry, the usual Jewish immigrants who, having established their place in society, hung on to it, like Jews do the world over even today, rarely moving outside the places or away from the people they know. My parents were always referred to by their nicknames, Mossy and Cissy, but my grandfather was referred to as the Tailor, which I found out years later: his name had been changed, as happened to many immigrants on entry to a new country. His original name was Bondel, which meant 'tailor' in Kiev where he came from. I wonder how an official interpreted Bondel as Feldman!

SCHMECKIE; NOUN:
PERTAINING TO A DONKOW,
USUALLY ENGLISH IN ORIGIN.
HAVING EYES OF UNUSUAL
PROPORTION AND MYSTIQUE.
SOMETIMES FUNNY.

I have often thought about my ancestors' decision to leave their homes for a better life far away. It seems the choices were few: London, specifically the East End, or New York, either the Bronx or Brooklyn. Like Mel Brooks's family before mine and Woody Allen's shortly after, those people made the decision based on weather, cost, relatives or something. I could have been Woody's cool one-year-older neighbour and we could have bonded with our interests and the like.

I've been a vegetarian ever since I first realised I had been eating dead bodies. When you're a kid living in a city, the only animals you see are dogs, cats, horses and birds (mostly pigeons). After I was evacuated to the countryside, during the war, when I was around five or six, I was introduced to other animals that I learned to love. I lived on a farm where the army was billeted and they would kill those lovely animals all day long. They slaughtered rabbits, chickens, pigs, cows and even little lambs – the ones I had just met. When I next saw meat on my plate, I realised someone had taken a life away, maybe even a friend's, and I have not eaten meat since. Over the years, I have tried to rationalise this: people have told me lots of reasons why I should eat meat, but it all comes down to eating the bodies of former living beings. I am quite sure I would not be a vegetarian if I had been raised in a primitive society, where it would've been essential to go out and kill an animal to survive, but I don't live in that society, and I have other options I can pursue in order to survive.

Being a vegetarian at boarding school was rough. When the teachers put meat in front of you it was expected that you eat it. In my case they knew I was vegetarian so they stood over me and tried in vain to force me to eat it. Being beaten and made to clean up my own vomit only strengthened my will towards vegetarianism. This went on every day. Sometimes when they weren't looking, I would smuggle the food into a handkerchief and store it in my pocket. As I was supervised everywhere I went, I would end up with rotten meat in my pockets until I could go to the toilet. More often than not, I ended up being sent to the dormitory, my clothes reeking of decaying meat, standing bare-arsed, trousers down, awaiting a thrashing from my carer. We also had to get our own slippers out so they could use them to whack us. We would wait and wait: the master would take his time coming along the corridor, his echoing steps slowly getting closer, and I knew he enjoyed every step. He would really thrash me with my slippers. My parents thought they were helping me by buying the best leather pair they could afford. Poorer kids were lucky because they had felt ones. I kept pleading with my parents that I didn't want new slippers, but they only wanted the best for me, and I knew it would hurt them to know I was being beaten, so I'd wear the slippers in as much as I could before the term began.

I learned how to masturbate at the same school. I was about ten and the whole dormitory learned at the same time. There was one kid who had been in reform school the year before and knew how to do it: he taught the rest of us. We were all fascinated and when darkness came he instructed us all to grab our cocks and jump up and down. All you could hear was the creaking of the thirty-two beds and their many springs. This went on for ten minutes or so, and because he didn't tell us how to come, most of us ended the term with really sore cocks. Nobody would dare ask or talk about it for fear of being beaten. Sex education was not on the curriculum, which in a way I'm relieved about: who knows what they would have told me and left in my head?

Later I read about Portnoy: how had he got to know about it and I hadn't? A good Jewish lad at a good boarding school had learned how to wank way before I did. Again, another coping skill that would've been a lot more useful and fun than Latin.

Any child could get into those boarding schools as long as their parents had enough money. At that point in my life, my parents did have enough money. We went through a kind of vast money spectrum: from absolute poverty to relative comfort. Years after I left home they were doing well. When I was born, my parents skipped digs and borrowed money just to get dinner on the table on Friday nights, the big night for Jewish families.

When the war came, my dad was sent to drive ambulances in East Ham, and then into the army, so we didn't see him for long stretches. While he was gone my mother continued to work in the markets, as they had both done before the war. It was the line of work that all immigrants seemed to follow. When the war ended my dad put his demob gratuity into a small manufacturing business in the East End, and within three years had become relatively wealthy, all due to his tremendous business acumen and the goodwill that was afforded to England after the war. He had become wealthy through his clothing business. He started off selling piece goods, material by the yard, and ended up owning one of the biggest gown-manufacturing firms in London, long after I had left home. He died without a will. He was extremely wealthy, as far as we all knew, yet when he died, aged sixty-four, we found out that his money was all tied up in the business, and his business wasn't worth as much as he had thought. The financial markets had changed and post-war good-will was fading fast.

My dad and I were so alike, which is strange because we misunderstood each other in many ways yet had the very same instincts. He was never a confrontational or political person and would shy away from discussions about anything that didn't pertain to his work or family matters.

We made the same mistakes, which we never learned from. We worked too hard, to the peril of all else. He worked for the sake of working. He hated idleness, so we never took it personally that he didn't spend much time with the family. He simply hated not having something to do. This more than rubbed off on his son.

He was without doubt the best natural comedian I had ever met. He also looked a little like Groucho Marx, which helped. He didn't smoke cigars, but he had the moustache, the glasses and the most natural wit I had ever come across. He hated the idea of me becoming a comedian. He could make people laugh with one look but felt this was not a dignified profession.

I tried working for him after I left school for the last time. We were like Jekyll and Hyde, the same person with opposite halves. He was a brilliant natural mathematician, and I had a knack for writing. He would instantly compute difficult figures in his head but didn't always know the best way to express his vision, vocally or in writing. I hated business and loved him for his wit and kindness. Most comedians I have met on my travels have told me they have had either a really bad or no relationship with their mum or dad or both. That was not the case with me: my dad left more of a mark than my mum did on my personality – I wanted to be a version of him.

By the age of twelve I was terribly efficient in Hebrew, partly because of my love of language but also because it was a good way to connect with my parents. It has not been much use to me but I knew my parents would be proud, and it became a key for me to understand them. I had learned Hebrew and Latin from this loony teacher, who had one leg and would hop around the place, like some Captain Grimes character. He was a one-legged genius and maybe because he was hopping around he got me interested. He would always say to the class that Hebrew and Latin were essential in life and then he would wink at me as if he knew I was on to him. Inadvertently, he was right, and again I'm grateful. So, too, were my parents.

I started as a comic, I suppose, playing in that English teacher's ENSA shows. It puzzled everybody, and no amount of Hebrew could suppress my parents' unease with my new-found passion. Most other kids had footballers or movie stars as their heroes. Mine were the great comedians of the time, like Sid Fields, Laurel and Hardy, Danny Kaye and later, but most importantly, Buster Keaton. My dad took me to see Danny Kaye at the Palladium when I was eleven, little knowing what a profound effect the experience would have on my life. As soon as I could afford it, I bought myself a brown herringbone jacket, brown trousers, and fashioned my hair into a Danny Kaye style. Quite handsome, for a lad about town, if I do say so myself!

I also saw Sid Fields around this time. I played truant from school in Luton to see *Up In Arms* at the cinema. I overdid the truanting by seeing it more than twenty times and finally got expelled. I was expelled from my next school for doing the same thing, except that time it was Denis Compton, the cricketer, and I was avoiding the sadistic, brutal masters in my school by seeing him play at Lord's every single day. Danny and Denis never knew that they'd got me slung out of school for looking dapper and trying to make my mates laugh!

My only sporting achievement was catching Denis Compton's ball at Lord's. All of us kids were allowed to sit along the grass at the edge. I was about six and the ball quite literally landed in my lap – the fact that it was over the boundary line didn't matter. Cricket was intriguing: nothing seemed to be happening and suddenly people would be leaping around in shared ecstasy.

I still have lots of sporting ambitions but they have little to do with the actual sport. I want to walk the wicket at Lord's. I don't want to play. I just want to walk out there, putting on my gloves as they do with such class, adjust my cap a little, look around, put the crease down. That's all I want to do.

I have included many sporting sketches in my shows through the years. I even got to do a good cricket sketch.

I have a very obsessive personality and sports of a certain ilk have always caught my interest. I find it fascinating to watch great athletes, especially when it doesn't go quite the way they expect. I have no strong affiliations with individual sports people, with the exception of Muhammad Ali, but that is for many other reasons. Cricket and baseball fascinate me no end. I like to see all the crazy rituals and obsessive behaviour the players exhibit under duress. Tugging at shirts and caps, walking around the lines, making sure not to step on them. For me it's as interesting as the score. Often I leave a match not knowing the score.

LORD'S

To walk among these giants or even here
Upon their field
With nothing to gain but to breathe their air
This shall be my shield

I find obsession very funny. I tend to home in on details and obsess a lot. Whether or not it comes in comic or dramatic form, it feels to me that this is the true root of comedy. I became obsessed with football when my family moved to Luton. I wanted to play for Luton Town FC and would have done if my comedic calling hadn't nagged.

I have returned many times and consider Luton to be my first real home. I was having such a fun time, and feeling very loved, while shooting on the set of *The Muppet Show*, that I thought I would go there, back to where I had been beaten as a kid on a daily basis. Because of my football infatuation, though, I remember mostly the good things. Ah, perspective.

I was the only Jew for miles around and all the kids would put out stories that my dad sacrificed pigs at midnight, making us out to be the monsters of the neighbourhood. They had never seen a Jew till they saw me, and they would beat me up each and every day. I was seven. It wasn't long before they would knock at the door of our house and ask if Martin was coming out to fight. My mother got so worried about this daily event. I would fight every day after school, and most of the fights ended with me being thrown into the local pond.

I wanted to kick a football around and they kicked me around instead.

I later became a boxer in a very amateurish way and was actually awarded a prize for being the best loser. This became the story of my life. I won best loser not because of good sportsmanship, having been beaten, but because I kept getting up off the canvas, knowing that I was going to get knocked down again. They seemed to respond to and like this spirit. In one particular fight I fell down three times, and may have been knocked out three times, yet still kept getting up. My nose became a rubber ball, having been broken a few times. This started the process of defining my comic face so at least I got something out of it. I suppose it taught me I have staying power. I should've stayed down but, in some deluded way, I always thought my opponent would get tired or give up. Eventually the kids of Luton stopped beating me up. I'm still the best loser and still get up when I should have enough sense to lie down and stay there.

Winning doesn't interest me. I have never wanted to be better than anyone else in anything I have ever done. One of the reasons, I suppose, is that I have never had much chance of being better: I was never big enough, strong enough, and I had to learn to be better than myself the last time I did something. I was not interested in beating anyone, just getting better for myself.

I have won a few awards in my life, but hate the whole thing, the nonsense of saying that one work of art is better than another, whether it's comedy, music or whatever. I despise the companies trying to make a competition out of something like acting, with more than one actor being up for the same award when they were never competing to begin with. It's quite embarrassing, really. They should just put the award in a room, send the competitors in and whoever comes out with the trophy in hand is the winner. As my award for best loser I got a tie and a fractured nose. When I went home my grandfather took the tie but I still have my fractured nose. I boxed for the Jewish Lads Brigade, in the London division. I also played football for them, not because I had particular skills but because they wouldn't have had enough contestants without me. Two years later I played for the YMCA, so my religious affiliations are somewhat fickle. I would've played in an Arab league if they'd have had me.

I went to Manchester with the Jewish Lads and got as far as the boxing semi-final. I had the Star of David on my trunks because Alf Phillips was a Jewish East End boxer hero at the time and he always wore one on his trunks, so we followed his lead.

The East Ham area was famous for its boxers. Alf was one and I, sadly, was not. I used to shape up well in the corner and I would hear comments around the ringside – 'This kid's all right.' They even laid bets on me. The fact that the fight was over the moment the bell rang and I was strewn, like roadkill, on the canvas didn't seem to matter. I've always managed to look all right in the corner. If only it could start and stop there!

Opportunities come no matter what we do but if you are not aware of what you want to do, the chances are you will not be aware of the opportunity. I became a comic accidentally. I hadn't intended to become one – I've always gone at life sideways like a crab.

As I look back, I'm quite sure I had the opportunity to become a writer earlier than I realised, but I had been beaten in school over a poem they refused to believe I had written. Although it wasn't a good poem, it was considered too good for a kid with my apparent lack of self-discipline. I always confused my keepers – this was the early forties and the teachers were incompetent Edwardians but, still, youth fought the great fight. They would ask us to write an essay on what we had done on Wednesday afternoon, a half-holiday at school. Once I started I would quickly fill an exercise book with James Bond-type capers featuring me as the hero (of course), going to Germany and capturing Hitler, bringing him home to face his atrocities and receiving the Victoria Cross for my efforts. I had written a bloody novel and they hated it because, they said, 'You didn't do that on your half-day off.' To the dormitory I returned with my slippers, not the

Victoria Cross. My half-days off from school were uneventful: with that story, I was simply trying to stay awake and not bore my teacher.

As a result of my so-called education, I am now truly vulnerable, not because of the beatings by masters or schoolboys but because of the scars they left on my psyche through killing any joy in learning. Still, I use my vulnerability and want to keep it. I have resisted the shell that has tried to form around me: I want to see life *sans* blinkers.

Writing has been my constant escape.

> *My mind is musty like a long and dark*
> *Unopened room*
> *Cobwebbed and dusty, as ideas rust inside*
> *Fearful am I to enter*
> *Into the gloom*

Entertaining can get boring: it's a case of how entertaining the lie is. Nobody's autobiography tells the whole truth. If it did, it would read like a list of statistics. I'm sure that most of the autobiographies I have read, and I have read a lot, are full of lies. Lies are far more entertaining than the truth: that is why we tell them. Exaggerations are permissible lies. Without them, we would lack drama. I have no doubt that Hamlet was a boring person until Shakespeare gave him the *News of the World* treatment. Most of my life has been spent sitting in front of a typewriter, dreaming up lies, because I'm not living life. Fiction is lies, and life is often fictitious in our memory. As productive as Shakespeare and Bach, with all his bloody children, were, the lie was their only ally. However novel the lie is, it is based upon things you know. You lie about something you know about to make it more interesting.

Perhaps I should've started our journey here with a disclaimer: 'Beware! Within here may lie lies!' I mention this because I've been trying to remember some of the names of the boys who beat me and, through repression or maybe even a dodgy memory, I can't. So I must fill the page with *an* account if not *the* account!

I have always been suspicious of people who place too high a premium on honesty and I usually suspect their motives. I am well aware that what I think now may change tomorrow with a new set of circumstances: something may happen to make me see things in a very different light. I accept that I am a contradiction; this makes me suspicious of those who hold themselves to one absolute truth and would punish you for not seeing the truth that they believe. A marketable truth is a lie because as soon as one divides it by the lowest common denominator it becomes a lie. Maybe a certain detergent does wash white clothes whiter. The question is, whiter than what? Everybody's clothes are washed the whitest, so somebody is lying.

PUTTING DESCARTES
BEFORE THE HORSE

I am, therefore I think – me, existence before essence.
There is no God and so far I have not had to invent him.
If I do, it will merely be that I cannot continue
Without the convenience of a cosmic scapegoat.
The only crime is to tamper with nature's equilibrium
That which we call evolution.
Murder is only a by-product of the greater crime.
Feed the hungry,
Bandage the wounded
And stand a cool guard on Evolution.
Why is for children and how is for adolescents.
The only questions left for adults are when and where.
Admit that logic rules and you admit the right to murder
Since logic brings with it the word 'necessary'.
Necessity is not only the mother of invention, but of its twin
Destruction and logic and will act as accessory before and after the
murder.
So sing loudly and you will drown your own screams.
Death is the only final now.
I hope I live to see it.

All religions claim to be telling the truth so all other religions, by definition, are lying. Every Christian is calling every Buddhist a liar and vice versa. The Jews are indeed liars but we are pragmatic liars. We have learned to make palatable lies and have even changed our names and identities to fit in. Again, it goes back to basic survival. The entire concept of nationalism is another lie: I would never fight a war to defend a piece of land. To defend myself and my family, yes, but never to defend anyone else's ideology.

I left school at the age of fifteen. I knew I'd learned nothing that would help me cope with the world. I could not matriculate so I forged my final report. I erased things and inserted my version of how well I'd done. I always wrote, 'Should try harder,' because I knew my father would not be too angry with that and it seemed believable, even though I had tried to work harder. It also meant I had potential, which I did, but the masters never knew or cared.

I never realised my academic potential and I could've tried harder but the incentive to do so was simply not there. There was no reason why I should. To get nine points out of ten, be patted on the head and then to be told I was a good boy? To hell with that! I didn't want to be a good boy or a bad boy.

I wanted to be a clown. I have always been and still am a clown. Back then it was for the boys or my mum and dad, and now it's for all to see on screen . . . Potential realised. As clowns or jesters, we're allowed a certain status that permits us to get away with insulting the establishment – to a point, of course.

Before my time the breaking point came when the king ordered, 'Off with his head!' after the jester had gone on too long or wasn't fulfilling his purpose. Nowadays the public is king and they have a knob on their telly to get rid of our heads. I am still a court jester and the hump on my back, one hopes, won't become a smoking time bomb – as long I'm being funny or at least bloody trying. At the very least I may avoid danger.

When comics become serious they are dangerous and, like poor Lenny Bruce or my dear friend Spike Milligan, that can lead to dark times: they lose the public's trust and leave them confused. I feel like I'm somewhat in this company of authentic loonies. We get away with saying pertinent things but are able to hide in the guise of eccentricity. The hypothetical is a great friend to us all.

I had no idea what I was going to do once I had left school. I wanted to write funny things. I had written funny things, essays and the like. My father had very different ideas. He wanted me to get into a respectable profession and, after much deliberation and deduction, he decided that advertising would suit. I got a job at an advertising agency delivering copy and blocks all around Fleet Street. Aside from my brief stint with my father at his work, this was my very first job.

At the same time I was doubling as a trumpet player at a lunchtime jazz club. I'd got my first trumpet when I was about fourteen and bought it on hire purchase. I'd thought that, magically, I would blow into it and the right note would flow out. As it turned out, my fantasy became a reality. I was a small Jew, who could just about get one note out of the thing, but nobody wanted to know. Turned out that musicians can be very unsympathetic and maybe even more so than your average person. However, as I hung out with them more and more I was taught choruses and was eventually allowed to sit in on sessions.

The night before I started at the advertising agency I had an overwhelming feeling that not only was I going to be a great jazz trumpet player I was actually going to be Miles Davis. When I awoke the next morning, much to my chagrin, I was not Mr Davis. I collected myself and decided that, at the very least, if I kept banging away on the trumpet I would become so good that I could make other people believe I was him.

Ever since, I have been on the fringe of jazz. I took two formal lessons from Phil Parker, who taught me technique stuff, and I was off and running, loving every minute as I got closer to becoming Miles Davis. It wasn't long before I became a professional. This didn't mean I was any good but what I lacked in talent I filled with passion and studied everyone I could. If you're a professional and you worry about the minimum standard of what you do, you may never reach any heights of skill or achievement in your chosen game. I never argued with anyone who complimented or encouraged me. Why make them feel bad by saying they're wrong? Music affected everything I did. I became the youngest bandleader in England at only fifteen.

(I also became the youngest published poet at the same age and later I was the youngest comedy writer in my circle. I've been the youngest in a lot of things. If only, like my heroes Charlie Parker or Danny Kaye, I had also been the best at what I did. Oh, well. Luckily I didn't get to see Dizzy Gillespie play until 1953 at the Rex in Paris: if I had seen him play earlier, I would never have called myself a trumpeter or even pretended to be one. It would have been similar to saying I was a dancer like Nureyev! I, too, had two feet, but that was as close as it would ever come.)

I had a semi-professional group called Marty's Gin Bottles. I fitted a bottle of gin into my trumpet case for effect, even though I hated gin and always have. It made me puke, yet I would resolutely drink it because I'd read Bix Beiderbecke drank it. I even thought that, by some process of alcoholic osmosis, the mere presence of the bottle in my case would turn me into Bix, a tragic destiny at such an early age. I thought that by being drunk or high great things would happen in my performances. They rarely did, although I have got some good laughs from my trombone work. The gap between your head and the bell of your horn is immense: what you think you hear and what the audience actually hears is tremendous in its disparity.

I spent some of my ad-agency lunch breaks in record shops that let you listen to a record before you bought it. There was a lovely bloke who worked in a store on Tottenham Court Road whose name was Beezer. He took a shine to me and we would listen to all the bebop and big-band heroes, and chat endlessly about the music and what each player must be like. He would tell me all the places to hear good stuff and invite me to concerts at higher-class venues. We saw Count Basie at the Palladium, and Sarah Vaughan, Ella Fitzgerald and Billie Holiday at the Flamingo in Soho, where Beezer introduced me to the owner, Jeff Kruger, who was really encouraging to anyone who claimed to be a player. I even washed glasses there in order to see shows. I first met Ronnie Scott at the Flamingo and would offer to carry his sax for him. He was part of a house band and they were as cool as it ever got.

This was the beginning of my real education in life. Beezer and I chatted about music and birds, and we relished every minute. There was a long ban on musicians coming to England – some union shit that I never understood. We'd go to house concerts, and Beezer would be asked to bring along some of the store's collection to kill time before the arranged act would play. House concerts were often hosted by rich people, and Humphrey Lyttelton or George Webb, two established jazz pioneers, would lead the guests into a jam and I could be seen hovering high above them all in a daze in Funland. I remember Fats Navarro and Art Pepper at one of these gigs, which were among the best shows I have ever seen. I also started to rub shoulders with people who would later become close friends. Now we still talk about how great those shows were and how lucky we all were. Eventually venues like the Eleven Club on Oxford Street and later Ronnie Scott's became the places to see great stuff. They were both owned and run by musicians, which made it even better to hang out there.

(My mate Beezer died in a tragic accident one New Year's Eve: a drunken barrister's car hit him while he was walking on the pavement, carrying a pile of records to a gig. I didn't know what had happened to him until after his funeral, and was angry that there was no investigation because he was an illegal immigrant. I still miss him.)

At the agency, I soon became a production assistant. I had a few small accounts and was doing quite well. I spent the lunch breaks when I wasn't in record shops looking for jazz sessions at clubs or the nearby polytechnic – or any place that would have me. I was like a bird released from its cage and could have fainted at any moment with the excitement of life and not being held captive at school.

It wasn't long before I was ditching the agency for days on end. We would finish a jazz session, then go to someone's party and there would always seem to be a bird around or someone who would lead us somewhere else. I would end up in Margate, when I should have returned to my desk a couple of days before to tap out addresses on envelopes. Instead I'd turn up eventually, full of Benzedrine, all hung-over and smelling of God knew what, with a trumpet case under my arm and raving about Charlie Parker.

My boss at the agency was a Quaker, a very serious and somewhat sorrowful man. This was an era when Quakers ran several ad agencies in London and before the introduction of commercial television. He called me into this big, beautiful, Quakerly office and, through a very tortured process, gave me every opportunity to be the one to say, 'The end,' even though he was completely justified in firing me. I don't think the poor man had ever had to dismiss anybody before and to see him going through the motions was harder for me to take than the actual loss of the job. He did his best to make me understand that I was and never would be interested or good at it. I was clearly not considered responsible enough to work at any advertising agency, in what was, ironically, one of the more irresponsible professions.

Since then I have been fired from many jobs and in every single case my employer was right.

My sixteenth year was the most educational eyE-and-every-other-bodily-opening period of my life. Once I'd left the agency, everything happened fast. I was spending all my time hanging out in Soho. In the late forties and early fifties it was the melting pot of the world and everyone seemed to hang out around the many amusement arcades on Charing Cross Road. It was a meeting place for every race and creed. Every nationality and sexual orientation would mingle, hustle and be on the move. I became obsessed with it all, as is my wont, hanging out with great people much older than myself and learning everything I could. It was also very frightening because there always seemed to be fights and I would spend every minute trying to avoid them. It was the complete opposite of hanging out with musicians, who were always sweet, encouraging and terminally broke.

There was a guy called Big Harry, who used to arrange group-fights every weekend. He was from Elephant and Castle, and every Saturday night his team would get together and fight their rival gang. It was almost like a football match in its format, but without a ball and with more fights than a Celtic v. Rangers fixture. They were very serious fights: broken bottles, chains, the whole lot. He would always find me and tell me to come along. I seemed to spend most of my days and nights avoiding him and his invitations, but, like the damp, he was always there. At first I thought it was all chat and that they were playing, like Brando's boys in *The Wild One*, until I saw them at it. They would fight for more than an hour, and whoever didn't go to the hospital would end up in the pub buying drinks for everyone well into the Sunday hours. I went along once, following far behind, hoping not to be seen but tracking them.

It was the early Teddy Boys era. I was never into any of that, too busy trying to be a black jazz musician. I wore peg-topped trousers and a pork-pie hat, which for a Jewish vegetarian was rather bold and hypocritical. But youth cuts corners for fashion. I continued to spend a lot of time in record shops trying to see what the greats were wearing on the covers of their records. They all smoked and looked bored, so I quickly followed suit. I fashioned a look that lasted for many years, often augmenting the same suit with a splash of colour here and there. My quest to be Miles Davis never let up!

I used to hang out with a bunch of Swahilis and, though I couldn't speak their language, I learned how to swear like them. Once again I was hoping that, through the miracle of osmosis, I would appear black and cool. I learned pretty fast that unless you were extremely talented there was no market for white black people. The blacks didn't want the whites, and vice versa, and the Jews didn't want either.

Being a misfit has always suited me and has always been interesting. Aberration is a nice place to visit but I wouldn't like to live there. Like a latter-day Jewish alcoholic Rimbaud, I wanted to experience everything my body could take. I believed that if I were to assimilate all possible experiences, like drugs and alcohol, I would regurgitate them in the form of art, be it music, painting or dodgy poetry. I was writing poetry and painting, and had become quite bohemian. I was convinced that if I drank enough I could write like Dylan Thomas, and if I took enough drugs I would blow like Miles or Dizzy. As soon as I learned that booze and drugs had actually destroyed many of my heroes' lives and stunted their creativity, I tried to slow down. Adolescence has the gift of an inability to see or experience life on a deep level: it became more desirable to *be* a poet or a musician than actually to write or play.

The lifestyle is the manifestation of the artist, not the totality. The vomiting poet I knew as Dylan Thomas was not the great man who wrote the poetry but, rather, the after-man. He was a vomiting drunk who once threw up all over my suede shoes in a Soho pub when I was still a lad of fifteen. I would watch him, as others did, and foolishly try to emulate his ways, drink too much and, like the idiot himself, puke everywhere and anywhere, piss in the middle of the street and strike out at anyone who came near me.

Brendan Behan – I got to know him for a while – died trying to live the lifestyle of the writer rather than spending his life writing, as he should have done. These brilliant talents left quite the wrong impression on us youth.

I think there is a kind of person who looks for magic elixirs, in drugs or booze, to enable them to do extraordinary things. Some take too long to realise they don't help and others run out of time. When I became a comic it took me a while to grasp that drinking before a show would slow or stunt my reflexes. At times I was hitting all the spots but the reverse was too often the case. I consider myself to be very lucky in doing whatever it is I do, especially writing, but I was luckier to survive the pitfalls.

I drifted through about a dozen strange, peripheral jobs. I worked for a couple of days as a smudge-boy for a street photographer. He was an African giant, almost seven feet tall with tribal scars on his face. I had never held a camera in my life. The job didn't last for either of us because although I tried hard to get him customers they would run into traffic to get to the other side of the street and avoid him. There weren't too many Africans living in London at the time, never mind giants with scarred faces.

I worked for a while in a musical-instrument shop for a lovely old bloke called Arnie, who fired me for giving free reeds and mouthpieces to my musician friends. He had a pretty good jazz record collection and the place would be full all the time with nobody buying anything. He was trying to make a profit and, though he liked me, he gave me the boot after my second warning. The retail biz was my dad's chosen field and was fast becoming the opposite for me.

THE WORM

Pity the common or garden worm
He has no legs he has to squirm
He has no scales, no wheels, no wings
He has remarkably few things
No means at all by which to travel
Except to ravel and unravel

Self portrait

By a weird series of events that I still don't understand, I ended up at Hornsey Art School doing evening classes long before the place was considered cool. I was working in the daytime at a bookstore near Baker Street, and before I got fired for telling people where to get better deals on books, someone entered me for a scholarship, and I won.

I had always loved drawing and really wanted to learn how to paint. At primary school I was beaten on the hands with a ruler for drawing in my jotter so I stopped for quite a long time. At art school it wasn't long before I came up against further obstacles in my quest to be a painter. My teacher insisted that I use a ruler when drawing perspective. I insisted that I wanted to paint flat and not rule the lines off into the distance, like he wanted. I argued that Utrillo painted flat. He pointed out that I was in no way close to being Utrillo. He also insisted that you can't invent your own perspective, like Van Gogh. We could only paint by the learned Hornsey method. When he heard that I had been telling other students he was full of shit, the axe came down.

I met a really hot bird there. She was completely wild and as crazy as you can get, obviously not all there. After the first night at school, she invited all the boys in the class, about nine of us, to her sister's house for blow jobs. She had been looking after the place while the sister was away. I was sure I'd misheard her – and I was the only one who showed up. I was looking for a place to crash and was up for anything.

I didn't expect her mouth on my cock so fast, and was surprised to feel one of her fingers in my bum at the same time. I don't know where she learned it all – she might have invented it – but as soon as she wasn't looking I took my leave through the bathroom window in fear of falling asleep and waking to find my cock had been sacrificed for a religion of her leaning.

The only thing I learned at the art school that inspired me was that Rossetti used to write poems at the bottom of his paintings. So I started doing the same, and felt that in many ways things were literally coming together for me.

I was meeting a lot of people, mostly artists of varying degrees of notoriety. This gave me more confidence. One was a real lad-about-town. He introduced me to John Minton, the painter. Even though I didn't know who he was at the time, I figured I could learn more from picking his brain than sitting for years at an art school. He was not only the first painter I'd met but also the first pop artist. He painted James Dean's death scene and exhibited it at the Royal Academy where people were outraged, Alfred Munnings among them.

Minton had a major talent and, like many great artists I've met, he knew it. Without my knowledge, he took one of my awful paintings to show to his good friend Dylan Thomas in a pub. Apparently he pointed out the poem I had written at the bottom. To my complete shock, he told me that Thomas had liked it and even said I should write. I believe that Thomas liked my poem because it was basically a rip-off of him and he was flattered. Before I knew it, he had shown it to his publisher at the Coach and Horses pub in London's Soho over, I am sure, many drinks, and bullied him into publishing a collection. At the age of fifteen, I found myself published as a poet. I loved the idea of seeing myself in print, though I immediately felt vulnerable because my stuff was now open to criticism.

I was not ready for honesty. One needs some illusion at that age and poetry gives you nowhere to hide.

The poetry I was writing was sort of skeletal, rather elliptic, once I had stripped all the thought off and, as per his suggestion, all the Dylan Thomas-style adjectives. They were raw poems that I was embarrassed by, and the exhilaration of being published didn't last long. I never published any more poems because I felt like I'd been caught naked in Piccadilly Circus at lunchtime, everyone jeering at me and nowhere to run or hide.

Very dramatic, I know, but to this day I still have nightmares about it.

The experience toughened me, too, in a very different way from school or being beaten up by the Luton boys. I soon got involved in all sorts of villainy.

Sustained by Joy
The Cosmos
Hangs in nothingness
A silver veil riddled with Black

I put in a brief stint working in a boot factory in Leicester. My job description was vague but my work was sadly very specific. All I did every day was to run the sole of a boot around a machine, which made a groove around the entire edge of the sole. I would then pass it to the bloke on my left. I never got to know or care what the guy on my right or left did but their faces were switched off. I soon got the jips being stuck between those two heavy-breathing stiffs. Even though I got good at rounding soles, I quit in the hope of spending more time with people who had soul, my jazz pals. I'd lasted three months.

In Leicester I fell in with a bloke who asked me to join him in his Red Indian fakir act. I became a Jewish Red Indian. A flurry of things happened at that time. I met Joe, a Hawaiian bloke, who was totally frightening with frizzy jet-black hair and a maniacal smile. He always carried a huge knife with him and made sure that everybody could see it. He introduced me to weed – this was soon after it had come to our fair shores. We would walk around smoking it openly and people thought we were smoking imported fags. We used to go up to coppers and ask them for a light. They had no idea.

The poor bastards had orders to crack down on homosexual activities and now they were chasing something they knew even less about.

Joe the Hawaiian also found a job with the Red Indian and we left Leicester for Dreamland, an amusement park at Margate, where we'd got a booking as a sideshow. In England at this time nobody knew the difference between a Hawaiian, an African and a Red Indian, so anyone with exotic looks did well, as long as they weren't too hurt by the racial insensitivities of the day. Joe was a boxer of some repute, and a roommate of Roger Moore at one point, well before Mr 007 made it.

The Red Indian fakir called himself Tayowana. His real name was Jack Taylor, and he came all the way from Peterborough, in Cambridgeshire, but was billed as 'Tayowana the Red Indian Fakir from the Rolling Hills of North America'.

The finale of his act was truly unbelievable. He would get into a large tin box painted with dragons – he'd bought it from a bankrupt magician – and while a band played 'Land of Hope and Glory', he blew himself up. He used real explosives and you could smell his burning flesh. They actually moved the candy-floss maker closer to us to camouflage it. Whenever I think of Margate the smell of candyfloss and burning flesh is in my nose. It was such a weird act. One of my duties as his assistant was to shoot arrows into his stomach from only four feet away. There were four eight-inch prongs at the end of each arrow and they would go into his stomach. He would just stand there quivering. He had visible holes all over his chest. He was quite mad: he used to jump up and down on broken glass as we beat him with burning clubs. Then, as he sizzled, we played bongos.

Hawaiian Joe, another Jewish lad called Johnny Myers and his West Indian wife Kathy, Jack Taylor from Peterborough and

I were Tayowana and Co. Jack used to stand in front of a mirror in his digs with his Indian headdress on and, method-style, convince himself he really was a Red Indian. His audience would laugh at first but quickly settle into total confusion and would usually return at least once with chums to validate the madness they had either seen or imagined. He had a very strange accent, closer to South Africa or Australia than the rolling plains of North America. He would tell us we could do anything we wanted if we set our minds to it. God help us all.

Once you'd worked a show at Dreamland you ended up working all the stalls there. It was always a panic with people coming and going or not showing up. I worked the bingo tables and rifle ranges, where the sights were all fixed and more often than not the gun wouldn't work. If you were brave you stayed a whole season. Considering my past, I was surprised to find myself working in one place for so long, even though I didn't know what my day-to-day job description was. I got to know all the gangsters in the area – they frequented the place to push drugs or try to pull a bird.

Dreamland

I quit the place many times in despair but always wandered back: there was nothing else going on and this was the only job I wouldn't be fired from because they couldn't get anyone else to do what we did for as little as they paid us. It was full on abuse of child labour, and I was one of the older kids.

I was part of many different acts – I'd join anyone who would have me. Often I was with Joe, who introduced me to his pal Maurice Seller and later to Mitch Revely, who, like us, were great but not at anything in particular.

After we'd worked at Dreamland for what seemed ages, our transcendent act was offered a small tour of minor music halls, which turned out to be major shitty halls. Places where signs backstage read 'Keep All Personal Items Off the Floor Because Rats Will Eat Them'. We had a lot of props stored in great cabinets with dragons on them, and when we arrived in a town we would borrow wheelbarrows to transport them all to the latest shitty hall.

The whole act got seven quid a week, digs were thirty bob, and there were usually five of us. How we ever covered our costs is beyond me. On reflection, maybe I wasn't employed, after all.

I was so desperate to break into the business of show!

We used to scrounge dog ends backstage, and there were always fights over cigarettes and food. I had fights with Jack Taylor in the wings and it would often spill onto the stage. We did support for a nude act called *The Saucy Girls*. Jack and I often interrupted them with our scrapping while they were onstage, doing their various poses as the Lady of Spain or Helen of Troy. I was scared shitless before going onstage and would drink draught cider, as much and as fast as I could, then stumble out there and try to keep it all together. I would shoot arrows all over the shop and dip into the wings to vomit. I would burn myself when I lit the paraffin for the burning clubs.

It's a wonder I didn't blow up with all the alcohol I had in and about me.

Perhaps at the age of fifteen, I didn't have enough grounding to be a good alcoholic. Maybe it's a thing that comes later in life, like being a monk, more of a vocation type deal. I certainly have given it a go on occasion!

It was a disastrous act that folded somewhere outside Leicester, us all taking our fights onstage with total disregard for the audience if there was one. It usually ended with the Hawaiian threatening to kill us all with his bloody big knife.

Towards the end of our stint, a really loony Scottish bloke joined the troupe. He was an ex-merchant seaman, a real toughie with tattoos over his entire body, balls and all, as he liked to announce. His whole philosophy in life seemed to be: ink your skin to show you're tough and never be caught sober after ten in the morning. Anyone who didn't abide by his fixed philosophy was a poofter. He was as close to a dwarf as it gets and as wide as he was tall. He decided that I was the least ridiculous member of the troupe and wanted to mould me into a new comedy act he was getting ready to break. He planned to do a tour of working-men's clubs and had me rehearse in his dirty digs, a one-room dump in the middle of Leicester. I was terrified of him. He would look at me with his mean eyEs, lean in too close and follow every sentence with 'Are you with me?' Like I had a choice. He would give me a line like 'Guess who's in the Navy.' The crowd would have to say, 'Who?' and I would have to say, 'Sailor.' I told him I couldn't because it wasn't funny. He came at me, grabbed me by the throat and sprayed my face with spit while screaming Celtic slurs at me. He made sure I knew that he was the Word and that any other words would be provided. At the end of the first day of rehearsal he sent me to the shops for milk and I never went back.

*　　*　　*

There were so many jobs I did for only one day. I worked as a kitchen porter in a hotel during lunchtime, which was fine until the dishes came and needed to be washed. As a vegetarian, I couldn't face touching or even looking at the discarded meat. I could've cleaned up shit, but I couldn't face meat. When I left that job I bumped into Jack Taylor, who told me the Scot was looking for me and was really drunk. I made a quick decision to travel abroad and chose France because that was where the painters and writers went but, more importantly, I felt the Scot wouldn't trail me there because of all the poofters.

It was easy to travel to France back then: you could jump on boats and trains without paying by pretending that you had become separated from your family – you put on a panic face and told the man at the barrier you knew where they were, then slid on.

With my trumpet under my arm, wrapped in brown paper like Bix Beiderbecke before me, I took trains, a boat and hitchhiked until I got to Paris. I was almost sixteen. I spent more time in France than I thought I would, almost a year, before I was asked to leave.

I did so many jobs in France to stay alive and I can't remember most of them because I was either so hungry that I was delirious, or they were so bad that I repressed them. After a short while I became tout to an American GI sculptor called Speedy Pappofatis. Of obvious Greek heritage, he was studying at the Sorbonne. He was really good – apparently he ended up doing some work on the United Nations building – but couldn't sell anything. He was just like most GIs back then: they would spend their pay the moment they got it and find themselves in trouble. When he was signing his work his name didn't help so he either put 'Señor P' or scribbled 'SP'.

I would hang around bars and cafés, looking like a student, and would tell any American tourists I could find that I knew a very famous French sculptor who was selling his work off cheap in order to move on to New York. They would follow me back to his studio, and Speedy from Illinois would fake a French accent. He was thrilled finally to be selling his stuff and gave me a decent commission.

At the same time I worked as an assistant to a pavement artist who would do pastels of the *Mona Lisa*. I would scurry about with my hat, hitting on tourists to support the artist. It wasn't much but more than he made on the days I watched him and noticed people admiring his picture but walking by. I told him if I chased them down a bit they might throw coins in our direction. Alas, it was not to be.

At night I would hustle to play my trumpet in cafés. I was so bad and would always say to the rest of the band that they'd have to carry me a bit because my chest was weak from the TB. Once I got going, I added, I'd catch up. I ended up playing a regular gig at Honey Johnson's tiny club in Montparnasse. It was an American-owned-and-operated joint and this was my first paid professional gig as a musician. I worked there for about three months. I stayed with four other musicians in a hostel, right by the river Seine. I was and still am a Niagara of adrenalin, which must be channelled or it would just piss itself away at the foot of the Falls. (I don't always know how to channel it.) We would all take speed to suppress our hunger and keep us lively.

On our very first night Bucky, the new American hotshot bass player, took a horrible shit in the bidet, not knowing it wasn't a toilet. He spent the night trying to poke it down with a pencil.

I eventually had to quit Honey's because I had fallen for a waitress and was caught shagging her on a table in the kitchen by Honey who, as it turned out, was her dad.

Back in London I wrote poems to a girl who worked at a tobacco kiosk outside the cinema on Charing Cross Road. I never met her but I used to send her poems anyway. I constantly fell in love with girls I never met.

There was another bird called Kathy, who worked the Western Show in Margate. I used to hitch a lift from drivers of the Covent Garden lorries to Margate every other night just to see her. We would have a quick shag in the back of a car, lorry or wherever we could and I'd get back to London that night. She was my first intercourse girl, a lovely bird with big boobs, who would just throw me down and ride on top of me with her boobs crashing on and about my face. She was only fourteen and I could tell I wasn't even close to being her first. She would spit on my cock and tell me to put it in her bum so she wouldn't get pregnant and at the same time would ferociously rub her vagina, like she was trying to rid herself of pubic hair. She was a real sweetie.

There was a bird I knew in Paris who lived with another sculptor. She was every sixteen-year-old's dream, beautiful, wild, bohemian, the whole nine yards. I wrote mad poems about her and all her wild Frenchness. About a year after I got back to London I was again working for an advertising agency, delivering blocks. I couldn't believe it when I saw that bird on a bus. I introduced myself to her in my learned French and, to my dismay, found out she was just another scrubber from the East End. I've got to give it to her because she was living the dream in Paris, walking around with her hair a mess and wearing her boyfriend's shirt. Back in London she was in wedge heels and a tight pencil skirt, which made her hobble, her hair perfectly built up in a bun. This was my first experience of shattered fantasies but not the last.

All I know about cars is that some have the engine in front and in others it's at the back. My engine is at the back: I am driven and I go where that takes me, and it takes me to some very strange places. But I don't have any choice in where I'm heading.

Having returned from France, I didn't go back to living at home for the same reason that any Jewish lad of that age wouldn't: rebellion against security. Instead I lived in the middle of Soho Square with Ray Courtney, who thought he was Jesus – rather, he was convinced he was Jesus. Somebody had to be 'Him', so why not Ray from Vancouver, Canada? He was a deserter from the Canadian Army, who lived in a shared hut with a bunch of us in the middle of London. We would creep through these railings every night and sleep in this little hut on a rectangular patch of undergrowth. I always knew I would find a bench there, which was comforting. We ended up staying a long time before the council caught us, chucked us out and knocked down the hut.

Ray circumcised himself sitting in a café called the 91 on Charlotte Street, Soho, because Jesus was Jewish. He used the knife he'd eaten his fish with. I'm pretty certain Jesus didn't have chips with his fish. Ray was a hippie before they were around, a pioneer hippie.

Jesus of Nazareth was not a lawyer, a doctor or the kind of Jew my parents would've accepted. I mean, he was a saviour, running around in the wilderness with twelve other blokes. That kind of carry-on would never be tolerated in Hampstead Garden Suburb, where my parents had moved. I think the reason he was not accepted as King of the Jews was because he didn't have a proper profession – he wasn't even a carpenter, like Joe, his maybe dad. He should have had a brass plaque hanging outside his door reading 'Jesus the Saviour'. Let them know he was working on something.

So, Jesus of Vancouver ran upstairs, and when he returned, he had blood all over him and proclaimed he had circumcised himself. The bloke I was sitting with, Mad Bernie Tobias (who later killed himself, like a lot of people I knew back then), said we should call the law or an ambulance. The last people you would call would be the coppers – on the streets we inhabited they were the enemy. Ray/Jesus from Vancouver said that he didn't need an ambulance or the police: he was the Son of God and his dad would take care of him.

God apparently did take care of him because about three months later he was walking around fine. I saw Ray many years afterwards and, apart from his teeth, he was all there. Well, obviously not *all* there because of the circumcision. Someone *had* looked after him. It hadn't been ambulance men or the law, so maybe he was right about his dad. He had as much chance of being related or even close to God as the Archbishop of Canterbury has.

We used to hang around the Roebuck, which was a pub opposite a dance hall called the Paramount on Tottenham Court Road. There was practically no illegal stimulant that couldn't be acquired within a hundred-yard radius of that pub.

After the hut was destroyed I moved into Rowton House, a doss-house, donated by some rich Lord Rowton, whose portrait was the only nice thing in the kip. It was a dark, damp, miserable place that would charge you to stay for two nights but most residents were flung out for not paying. I moved home, and at first my parents were thrilled.

The night I returned I invited a few chums to come by and have a bit of a play. Things got out of hand in a hurry. The musicians, as always, were fine but the hangers-on got carried away and before we knew it a suburban orgy had broken out. The police were called because of the noise and a bloke fell out of a window onto broken glass and there was blood everywhere. Just as I was cleaning it all up, my parents arrived. It looked like a crime scene and they made it known in no uncertain terms that my friends, with their beards and bare feet, were not welcome in their household or, in fact, in the neighbourhood. I left home again: I had a new family, who weren't welcome in suburbia.

Of course I knew I could go home without them, but I couldn't live my parents' lifestyle and they couldn't countenance mine because it involved all kinds of disreputable carryings-on. In a way I felt I didn't belong anywhere and was just a temporary member of the human race. It took me about forty-three years to shake that.

I went back to Rowton House, where we had to tie our boots to the bedposts so they wouldn't get nicked or chewed by rats. We would lie there at night, everything hidden under the blanket for fear of theft, in that bloody awful dormitory, which hadn't changed in a hundred years. I lay there and wondered what basic rights we were being denied.

Poor people don't write about the state they're in. Retrospect is the only place you can write about it.

One night I was lying in my shitty bed, breathing in the stench of carbolic and damp and thinking it was the worst thing I had ever smelt, when the guy in the next bed pissed on the floor. The acidic odour soon reached me. I thought, Well, he couldn't hold it. He was a sad-looking case, and I just wrapped the blanket over my head until I was awakened the next morning by a scream. I was dragged from under the covers and barred from ever coming back. It turned out the crafty bastard had pissed under my bed. Getting barred by the Salvation Army is the point of no return.

My next night's sleep was in Green Park, me and my trumpet in its withering brown-paper bag. It sounds very romantic but do consider England's climate in winter. It got so bad I became almost giddy with the madness of it all. No part of me ever thought this would make for a great yarn to tell my pals later in life on the golf course. I would fall asleep and wake up again all night long but always rose at five and blew a kind of reveille with my trumpet that could be heard all over the park. As I played I could hear the rustling of startled figures getting to their feet and the park would be full of tramps.

I also slept in Waterloo Station because all you ever needed was a ticket stub, which was easy to come by. The ticket collectors were nice and would accept a blank piece of paper as long as I was nice in return. The coppers at the stations were easier on us dossers than the ones in the park. Waterloo was near the Sally Ann and there was a moving community of bums, many of whom I have seen in recent years. We reminisce about the good old days only because those days are now old. Most of the community didn't make it and others moved on, far and away.

At this time I never knew from one day to the next where I was going to sleep. Some sort of coping skill prevented me thinking about this all day until the time came to do something about it. I might wake in a mate's flat or on one of the bomb sites, then figure out whether I would go solo for the day or join up with whoever was around. We would pool our money and end up at some café in the East End.

Eventually I moved into a studio flat in Belsize Park with Hawaiian Joe and his big knife. He was a pretty big man and he would go for anyone who questioned his looks or actions. A husband and wife, both bisexual painters, also lived in the flat. Joe knew they fancied him and would play along for a place to kip.

Some good things came out of that period: good writers, good painters and such. In a way, my generation was in transition between old-fashioned bohemian and today's pop culture. We didn't give a shit about what we wore or how we looked. We grew up as Fabians and turned into pseudo-Marxists. We were always considered shadowy figures because we didn't fit in and regular people ignored us, either because we frightened them or they were too busy getting on with their own dramas. We were ahead of our time, but we were of our time. It was the end of the Soho scene and we were dedicated to revolution: it was important for us to spit at the system and behave badly, long before the punks existed.

Although it sounds like I'm glamorising it, there's nothing glamorous about the smell of damp and the effect it has on your body and mind over a sustained period of time. I would always scrape to dress well in order to give myself a chance. Often I would swap a suit with someone who had stolen one so I looked like I had means. I could have gone home and taken advantage of my father's fine linens but that thought never crossed my mind: I was hellbent on making a career in some sort of racket that I created for myself. Bound for Glory and a Rebel without a Clue was me.

I was an American for a while. The only way to pull a bird back then was to have money, the proper clobber and wheels, or to fake it as a Yank. I became an eighteen-year-old American because life as a bohemian sixteen-year-old Jew was very boring. Being an American gave me swagger and potential. I had mates who worked on boats or in the docks and they would bring me all sorts of great gear stolen from cargoes: short ties, cut square at the bottom; Argyle socks and button-down shirts. We had crew-cuts and hung around Piccadilly Circus tube station, pretending to be GIs on furlough. I had developed a quite convincing American accent, and was even smoking American cigarettes – a mate called Fat Stan threw illicit packs my way. (He knew I'd share them, thereby increasing his circle of dependency.) All this came as a complete shock to everyone who had hung out with us days before as bohemians, with long hair and sandals, but they knew we were doing whatever we could to get by – one guy even bought an American car and drove it around in the hope of pulling birds.

It wasn't long before I got tired of that caper – shaving alone drove me nuts.

It was 1952 and I decided I wanted to meet my hero, Charlie Parker, who was doing a run in Paris. A mate was going there to hitch up with a French bird he had got pregnant, so off we went, he to face domesticity and I to meet my hero. As I said, you want your heroes to be wonderful, superhuman, marvellous people. When I finally got to meet Charlie Parker, all he wanted to talk about was snooker. He was obsessed with it, to the extent that I couldn't figure out whether he liked or hated it. Maybe he was trying to figure it out himself, but he bored the crew-cut off me. Dylan Thomas only ever talked about how much he had drunk or could drink. Since then, when I've had the chance to meet one of my heroes, I've often made an excuse to avoid it. This has backfired on many occasions when I couldn't remember the lie I'd told to get out of it, or the lie had been changed by whoever passed on the message. I told Frank Sinatra's people at a Las Vegas show that I couldn't come back afterwards and meet him because I had a cold and feared it might be contagious. Sinatra was told I didn't agree with his politics, which might have been true, though I didn't know what his politics were. I just knew him as a great singer and interpreter and had loved him for years.

By the time I got to work with Groucho Marx he was an old man and I couldn't talk to him as the atomic or brilliant wit he had been: he was merely an old man dealing with decay. All he ever talked about was his bowels.

Anyway, after that short and disappointing trip to Paris, I moved into a new flat with Hawaiian Joe and a bloke called Jerry, who sold pot – 'charge', as we used to call it. We used to go out looking for trouble anywhere we could find it.

When you have nothing, it's easier to steal stuff from people because you don't know what it's like to lose something and therefore you can't put yourself in someone else's shoes, even if you've nicked them. I once broke into a car. It's like an O. Henry short story, really. It was Christmas Eve and I got pissed and found a car that was easy to break into. I found a few parcels on the back seat and took them with me. When I woke up the next morning I discovered I had stolen choirboys' surplices. I felt so awful that I returned to where the car was parked, found the nearest church and dropped them off with a note, saying I was sorry and something about having seen the light.

A couple of days later I went home to see my parents. As I approached the driveway, I saw what appeared to be a Bentley parked in front of their house. My first thought was that one of the gangsters I had worked for or stolen from had come for me. As it turned out my old man had bought himself a new car, a very flash one. At first I was embarrassed, but soon started feeling proud of him for overcoming so many obstacles to get to where he was.

This was a big moment for me. All I had ever achieved was passing my 11-plus exam on my second go and learning how to live and survive in the wild. I never wanted to be part of any establishment but couldn't help admiring how my dad had kept his dignity, done well and never rubbed it in anyone's face. He would give all the kids and neighbours a ride in his car and was always more amazed than all of them by his success.

It was around this time that I started to wonder if I could sneak into some sort of entertainment-type racket. I was writing funny things and could play a few instruments badly, but it was when I was clowning around that I could feel people finding time for me. I've always been surrounded by villains and have always liked them. I'd learned from them that if you don't have the stomach or bottle for crime, get out or you'll end up broken. I'd never had the bottle to be a villain but tried hard. I stole from Woolworths when I was ten, and my last job as a villain was driving a getaway car with no licence. Everyone else was riding high on adrenalin but I was sweating bullets and could've passed out with fear.

I'm a failed criminal but I found that most performers had something I could see in myself: our own form of bottle. Finding what you were good at was the shortcut to having an act.

After years of grifting and grinding, I noticed that I had a way with words and felt more and more that I wanted to write things down. I realised I had to focus on finding a way to make a living by becoming a really great writer. I had seen Danny Kaye at the Palladium, and he had set the standard in terms of the quality that I must attain. Now I was at the stage door trying to get jokes to anyone who opened it. At first I stole jokes from everyone else and tried to make them my own. Then I thought of Danny sitting on the edge of the stage, smoking and talking casually to the audience. A light went on in my head: I knew it took many years for a performer to be so at ease with his audience, but it was his straightforward Everyman dialogue that connected and his jokes felt like personal messages he had just thought of. He made people feel relaxed and up for anything he threw at them.

I started to read books about and interviews with the people I liked and could relate to.

I gravitated towards simple structures and spent time looking at various subjects, like religion, I could make fun of. I would write down as many things about my chosen subject that I thought other people would see but not think of as funny. More and more I found myself writing little jokes and stories on napkins or on any bit of paper I could find. I had pockets full of them and most of them were nonsense. I liked the really strange ones best. The abstract has never been a hard place for me to dwell in.

So much happened to me between the ages of fifteen and nineteen that I can't give a proper chronological account of it but on reflection I see that much of who I am now was moulded in those years, for better or worse. 'Whatever it takes' was my motto. I derived a certain high from hanging around with heavy-hitting villains but, along with the dead-end girls I was pursuing, the allure was lessening.

On my seventeenth birthday, I answered an advert in the *Stage* newspaper for a personable young assistant. It said to include a recent photo. I grabbed the only photo I had, a posed shot from my bar mitzvah when I was thirteen. I couldn't believe my luck when I heard back right away. I soon found my way to Exeter by train, full of excitement. I was met there by a huge man who looked like a latter-day Orson Welles in a fright wig. He informed me that he was a hypnotist and did a show. When we got to his car he introduced me to his wizened little wife. This was my first official foray into showbiz. We took a short drive to the caravan where they were staying. It was their residence while playing one-night stands in village halls. They both groped me on the short trip. That had never happened before! I soon found out that they had fancied me from the moment they saw my bar mitzvah photo. They didn't understand that I really did want to be in show business, so I spent most of my time beating off their advances between horrible shows and empty halls.

The thirty bob I'd thought I was going to make never materialised. My job was to hang posters in each town we arrived at, then try to drum up interest in those two fools. I would walk onstage and put a song called 'Legend of Glass Mountain' on a record-player. He would hypnotise his wife and then me. I couldn't even act like I was hypnotised, and his wife wasn't any better. I lasted almost two weeks. The end came when they tried to rape me in my sleep in the caravan, which was parked outside Guildford. I woke up with their smelly drunken bodies on top of me.

I managed to get out from under them and told them I was leaving. They threatened that if I ever told anyone what they'd done, they would blacken my name in the business for all time. I knew no better and ran, in the wee small hours, as fast as I could to get away from them.

I lived most of my life in the wee small hours. Villains and jazz musicians were rarely seen in daylight, but that didn't stop them wearing shades while they were doing their best work. It's difficult to do a gig or rob a house at eleven in the morning. What we did was best done clandestinely.

My family tree is stunted. We can only really trace back one generation and all we know from before that is that we came from a long line of peasants and misfits. I wish a spectacular type of person would pop out of that tree. I wish we were somehow related to Jack the Ripper or someone like him. We're so unlucky: as second-generation British Jews we can't trace our madness back. The Royal Family know how mad they are and revel in it. How lovely it must be to know that you're not the first potty one in your family.

I was getting to the point in my life where I felt I'd better bring a bird home to my parents, a girl who at the very least had a couple of eyEs, ears, and a mouth that didn't scream obscenities all the time. They were becoming more and more worried about me. I was looking increasingly daft every time I swung by to say hello, eat and bathe. They saw me as the family eccentric.

I hate eccentrics. I much prefer loonies, like Spike Milligan, who came from a long line of the type that thinks nothing of riding into a pub on a horse and ordering drinks. It's easy for Spike to step outside the norm, which is why he's been such a huge influence on me and on many English humorists.

My metamorphosis from writer to comedian happened because of Spike. When I first heard him on *The Goon Show*, it was as though someone had turned my life from black-and-white into colour. I was the result of an illicit union between *Take It From Here*, written by Denis Norden, the verbal intellectual Jew, and Frank Muir, the dilettante Englishman, and the rambling lunacy of *The Goon Show*. My parents and I enjoyed those shows, which brought us closer together, and I'm sure a lot of young people and their parents had the same experience, unlike the next generation with the Beatles. Perhaps my parents didn't quite get the humour of *The Goon Show* but laughing at lunacy is a great leveller.

There's a family tree of British comedy. Spike and the Goons drew from Edward Lear and Lewis Carroll, and the Pythons came after *Beyond the Fringe* and *At Last the 1948 Show*. Perhaps Barry Took and I were a hybrid of all those camps. A family tree shows us where we came from, how to use the tradition, and those who went before, so that we can try to put our own angle on it in the hope of connecting directly with our own generation. What I owe to Spike he owed to Stephen Leacock, and Leacock to Charles Dickens. God knows who came before him. Maybe Dickens was the first.

Spike and I read a lot, which reflects in our own writing. Other writers just scribble down what they've heard and learned in life. Writers and comics don't like to admit they're readers because it's a cop-out, relieving them of responsibility. They may even be labelled unoriginal. We all want to be immaculately conceived, owing debts to nobody, so I adopted a comic tree of my own to use as a reference.

On my return from Exeter and the crazy hypnotist, I began to realise my limitations as a horn player and decided to try the drums. I thought anyone could hit things and make rhythms – until I sat in the front row of shows with Buddy Rich and Jo Jones, but that was later. Out of the blue my father proclaimed that it would be a huge help for my career if I were to secure my own drum kit, and he helped me get one. Before I even got around to playing with it, a bloke named Flash Winstone, who called himself Professor Bebop and fancied himself to be the original of the form, asked me if he could borrow my drums for an audition. He couldn't get hold of his own set because his landlord had locked him out of his flat for not paying the rent.

I was flattered to be asked and felt as if I was now on the inside of the professional jazz players' club. I didn't see the bold

Flash again for two years. Meanwhile, I got into trouble with the hire-purchase company, the law and my father, who, in a kind gesture of support, had guaranteed the purchase of said kit.

Two years after this I was doing an act. We used to rehearse in the afternoon at a club owned by Jack Spot, a notorious gangster, in exchange for cleaning the place from the night before. The Blue Spot Club was in Soho's Old Compton Street. There were three of us and we were an instrumental act. I played trumpet, another bloke played clarinet, and the third played guitar.

One afternoon the clarinet player and I were jamming together while the guitarist took a leak. The clarinettist was playing the club's drum kit. A phone call came through to the day manager. He answered it, spoke for a minute or two and hung up. The call had been from Jack Spot, who was upstairs. He'd asked who was playing and the manager had told him we were a few of his chums rehearsing. Jack said we had 'swing' and instructed him to hire us and fit our band into the bill for that night. We were bowled over.

So, we were hired to do a multi-set gig every night – but we didn't have a drum kit. Then we found out that the club's regular drummer had just been fired. He turned out to be the esteemed Professor Bebop, one Flash Winstone, and these were my drums. I'd got my old kit back and a regular gig all in one afternoon.

We worked there for about four months, playing mostly for villains and the like, who would carry shooters tucked under their armpits. When they requested a song you'd bloody better know it or at least have a go at it. 'My Mother's EyEs' was a constant, 'That Old Black Magic' another. They treated us well because they knew we weren't any good but we were trying hard and we always laughed at their jokes when we were told to.

I worked in a bunch of clubs around this time. I got gigs filling in for other players. I even got a gig as a bassist. To this day I can't play bass. The bassist was ill so he asked if I would sit in for him and told me he'd lend me his instrument. When I said I would if I could play the bloody thing, he told me that no one listened and as long as I ran my fingers up and down the neck of the guitar and looked bored, it would be cool. The other two lads in the band went along with it but were visibly irritated when people bought me drinks and complimented me on my great work. I looked the part, in a sharp suit, thin tie, shades, a pork-pie hat and very shiny shoes. That was bottle, and how to use it!

This was when I realised I was outside the norm of my family tree.

I was game for anything and relished the challenges, so I can safely insert 'professional bass player' on my CV. I never played drums again after the run at Spotty's place. I could barely keep tempo for one song, never mind several every night. Most people who fancy themselves as a musician make the same mistake I did. I hear people say, 'I tried drums but they're too difficult.'

'All the more reason to applaud the good drummers,' I say.

Audiences are full of idiots like me who had a go at it and now know how hard it is.

As I've said, I had bands from the age of fifteen. Most of the members were great players. Tubby Hayes got his first job with us. Quite a lot of people I know and have worked with since then, like Dudley Moore and Johnny Speight, were around the scene back then. At one point we were called Marty Feldman's Bebop Seven and the band at various times included Tubby, Les Condon, Kenny Napper and a talented young singer called Lillian Klot, who would later become known as Georgia Brown. All were proper players. Lillian had a brother called John, who later became the first person to buy a joke from me, and Georgia became a great pal. We were hired to relieve Johnny Dankworth and his outfit at a place called the 52 Club. It was all bebop jazz back then and all great players, except me. I had bottle enough to blow every so often but most of the time I was just puffing out my cheeks and shutting my eyEs as tight as I could.

I used to tell people that not only did I lead the band but the compositions were entirely my own. I continued to tell everyone that I had severe TB and the doctor had instructed me not to play, but I couldn't not play: they bought it. Tubby has a recording of one of our shows from the early days – he said it was quite good and that you could almost hear me.

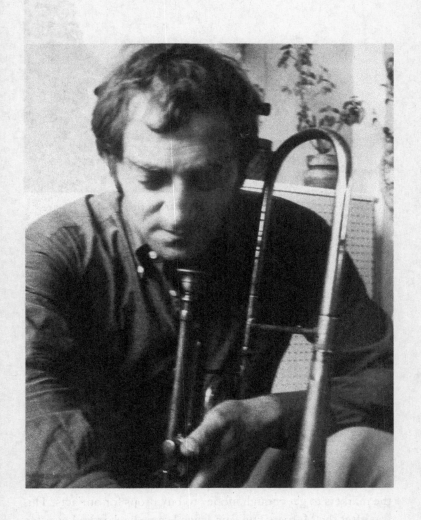

the picture to get emotional involvement in the deeper music. The
drumkit, that is an instrument that takes us back to primal energies.
Everything about it, from the physicality, and tends to keep us locked
into a kind of tribal vibration... so we don't do that.

Music is my therapy, my world away from this world. Few are permitted to enter my Secret Garden, and it is secret because I have no idea what I'm doing or how I'm doing it but for me, it's everything.

The Marty Feldman Bebop Seven was to be my escape out of the mediocrity and depravity of my current state, but soon the band split up and re-formed without me. I was left with a reputation as the worst trumpet player in London.

Around this time I somehow found myself at the Regent Theatre in Hayes, supporting an act called the Saucy Girls. Two mates, Mitch, a clarinettist, and Maurice, were available and willing to join in, and we had a provisional booking for one night. I still don't know how we got the job. We felt we ought to have costumes so we wore matching suits and ties with white scarves, white coats and black trousers. During the day we would work in the markets to get enough money to buy props for our acts. This was after the Margate Fun Fair, when I came back from Leicester, I reteamed with Joe the Hawaiian again, and the third was a clarinet player called Mitch whom we met along the way.

At this time I was on the periphery of a lot of different things. I was never really part of the Jazz revolution at the time, nor was I involved with Music Hall, we came around after Music Hall was coming to a sad end. I was entrenched on the fringes of it all.

People from that scene remember me as this idiot kid with a trumpet case under his arm or with a box of paintbrushes or carrying a journal filled with dodgy poems. I so desperately wanted to be in the scene, any scene at all. Joe's mom had been in a band called The Felix Mendelssohn, a Hawaiian band, where Joe had learned the ropes a bit and would be dragged by his mom into whatever she was doing at the time. He taught me *The Hawai-ian War Chant*. He played ukulele and guitar and would twirl his knife all about the place without any prompting. So with me on trumpet, and getting the new clarinettist, we figured this was enough to build an act on. We didn't have any shape or form and we did impressions of people that nobody knew. Joe did an impression of Farouk but nobody knew who King Farouk was, but Joe had dark skin and wore a fez and everyone bought it as authentic. He also did an impression that I later took over of Toulouse-Lautrec. As long as we were on our knees and had a beard it seemed to work and we would go out of our way to point out that it was not José Ferrer's interpretation of Toulouse-Lautrec but rather our very own impression of him, taking no notice of the fact that none of our audience had no clue of who he was anyway.

This became our strength, confusing these poor bastards who paid money to escape their mundane existence. It was a ragbag of bits and pieces that we threw together knowing that it was far from good. A good bloody mile from good, more like.

Joe saw the writing on the wall and was set on moving away.

He was always on the move and was initially part of Morris, Marty and Mitch but the Islands of Hawaii were a calling.

We did our new act for one night in Hayes, in a horrible grubby theatre, and we got paid off. The manager told us that the patrons had been insulted by our performance – it had lacked content – and demanded their money back.

This was the beginning of an act we decided to name Morris, Marty and Mitch. Morris and I had done stuff before this with Joe the Hawaiian, but Mitch had joined us assuming we were a legit musical act and that his clarinet playing could only reach the heights.

Morris, Marty and Mitch in action!

My eighteenth birthday was memorable. We were standing in our rented white jackets outside the stage door of the Cardiff Empire, trying to shelter from the pouring rain while we had a smoke. In the distance a poisonous dwarf was screaming at us. He kept pointing and directing all his rage at me. I said, 'What do you mean?' not realising that I was opening Pandora's box. He kept yelling something about my white suit. I found myself bending down so that I could relate to him, only to find he was intent on head-butting me. Morris tried to help me and the little fucker head-butted him in the face. Then, before we knew it, he had wee Mitch in a headlock with blood coming out of his ear. We had blood all over our white jackets and the police arrived. It took four of them to get the nasty little bugger into the paddy-wagon.

Just as they were driving away, we were called back to the stage by the manager to do our closing number with Harry Lester's Hayseeds. We stood arm in arm with the beautiful Kaye Sisters, who were also on the bill. This was the second show they had ever done and they were decked out in stunning yellow frocks. We all sang 'Walkin' My Baby Back Home' with blood dripping all over us. Mitch was crying because he was sure he had lost his ear. We ended up having to go to the hospital.

The next night, while we were doing an awful routine, featuring all three of us playing drums and singing 'Give Me That Old Soft Shoe', the pit band threw their shoes at us. I was knocked unconscious by their drummer, who aimed his hobnailed boot right at me. He would've been a good cricket bowler: he hit me full on from quite a distance.

We were hired at various venues to fill short gaps between costume changes or between acts, but often we were sent out and used as a barometer to test how hostile the crowds were. This would have been 1954 and the crowds were truly awful at those places. A year later, we got a chance to appear on a proper telly show and that audience was rough too.

I only stayed in the act because I needed to do something. I liked the blokes, and Hawaiian Joe joined us for a while. He specialised in kipping with landladies so we got free food and digs. He bailed out when he fell for a bird and decided he didn't want to travel for a while.

Nobody ever listened to any of our act and there was never enough money to go round us all so we had to find markets in the towns where we played and worked there in the daytime. Eventually we got a dodgy agent, who sent us out to all the number three and four theatres – outhouses, I called them.

We played Belfast a few times. Actually, it may have been the only place we had a genuine return booking. It had the nicest people of any town I had ever been to, but it was also by far the most frightening place I had ever been to.

Silver McKee ran Belfast like Capone did Chicago. He had several scars and strange skeletal formations. He had been a bodyguard to a fighter called Robert Cohen and was well known not to tolerate fools. During the Troubles, he ran everything, did business with both sides, Catholic and Protestant, and was a target to none because they needed him.

For some reason he took a liking to us, possibly because he did business with Jack Spot, who ran London in a similar fashion. After our show the word came to us from two very fit-looking blokes that Mr McKee wanted to meet us for a drink. We declined. The blokes chose to address Maurice by pressing him up against a wall, and while one leaned on him, the other said, 'Don't make life any harder on yourself, son.' It wasn't lost on the remaining two performers that they were leaning on the biggest member of our troupe. After the first show we were extremely happy to join Mr McKee for refreshments. He informed us that he was going to take care of the guy who had yawned rather loudly during our act.

We decided it best to agree with everything he said. He was a huge, burly man but gentle and mostly spoke in a very hushed tone. The ladies seemed to love him. He was always opening doors for them and asking after their families. He went out of his way to show us a good time in his city. He repeatedly told me, 'You are doing God's work, son, making these poor fuckers laugh.' I, of course, agreed. He would take us on his rounds while he picked up his rake-off from all his bookies – he controlled all the gambling in the city as well. One night the police were pursuing him: to avoid them he had us follow him through an elderly couple's house as they sat drinking tea. They didn't even look up from their newspapers, just said, 'Evening,' as he moved through their lives with his entourage.

Silver, like my hero Charlie Parker, had a passion for snooker and took us to his own club. I said I played but the other two cowards hugged the bar as I trembled my way through a game. While Silver was in the Gents, one of his employees pointed out the bullet holes in the ceiling – Silver's response to being behind in a frame. It turned out he had a very strong winning record.

As he drank we saw a very unpleasant side of Silver emerge. After I'd let him win for the third time he told us we were in for a treat. He was taking us to his mother's house for a bite – at three in the morning. First, though, we had to make a quick visit. When we reached a small tenement house, Silver told us to wait for a second while he checked in with a friend. We dutifully stood in the rain under a streetlamp. Suddenly we heard loud noises and Silver's voice, which had taken on an edge. We heard slapping, and in a flash, a man's body flew out of an upstairs window head first and crashed to the ground with a horrendous thud, right beside us on the pavement. When I leaned down to see if he was alive, one of Silver's thugs grabbed me by the shoulder and told me to mind my own business. We threw up all over the place and were told to pull ourselves together before the Big Man came out.

A bit later we found ourselves sitting around a table in Silver's mother's kitchen, waiting to be fed. She looked like Barry Fitzgerald in drag. She told us she was going to make us a fry. I knew I couldn't eat. I thought that night would never end. Luckily Silver didn't seem to notice me pushing the greasy bacon and sausage around my plate. His mother regaled us with stories of her son's kindness. After a long time, he told us he would see us back to our digs. His mother told him he would not and that it was past his bedtime. He didn't dare challenge her.

Many years later I was invited to play in a charity football match in Belfast, and though I really wanted to go, I declined! The fear was still within me.

Happy Xmas Parasites !!
from **Moris, Marty & Mitch**

Just got back from France

The French Press said :

" *Also appearing were Moris, Marty & Mitch* "

Throughout this time I was constantly writing, mostly little stories, about people who were hell-bent on not passing unnoticed through life: they'd make the best of it by any means they could. Not autobiographical, then! Speaking of biographies, back in my days of hustling to be a musician, I knew a bloke called Jack Hobbs, who was a good player, and later got into publishing with his wife. During my telly days he recorded a bunch of tapes of me chatting about my past with the idea of doing a book. He did one with Spike, but I felt I hadn't done enough to write about myself. Years later I found the tapes and was surprised by how vivid it all was: maybe that's the trick, to keep a journal.

We would audition for anyone who would have us. Most people didn't know what to think of us or what to do with us. At some point we even wore black tights in an effort to be different. The only offer we got came from an agent who had no intention of putting us up for anything. He liked the way we looked in tights and never made eyE contact with us. We told him to fuck off.

We finally got an offer to return to *Saucy Girls* as a regular act. We were told they hired us because we were versatile, which we knew meant they would have us do anything, even move scenery and announce the acts. It was the first time I was offered a percentage of anything – I didn't even know what that meant, but was led to believe we would be paid a lot of money. We ended up with about seven pounds a week to split between us.

The Dean family were basically the whole show. Derek Dean became quite a popular comedian and I learned so much from him. He was the show's musical director and had a great piano act. His daughter had a dog with which she did a knife-throwing routine. Mrs Dean stitched things for Wardrobe.

They didn't need anyone else, yet included us, and a boatload of chorus girls. The show ran for two years and they packed them in because there were nudes. We filled the gaps between acts by either helping people getting on and off the stage, banging a drum or getting pissed in the theatre bar. We did almost everything as long as it didn't take long. We always got big applause when we were introduced in the finale. That was the only time we were all on the stage together and we were convinced people thought we were someone else. While the other acts were on, we amused ourselves by frolicking with the chorus girls. We all slept with at least one, until their handler wouldn't let any of us near them.

In those days onstage nudes had to stand still: any movement was perceived as provocative. We often heard that someone from the Watch Committee was in the house to make sure none of the girls moved a nipple by so much as an inch. Margot was a lovely girl – I quite fancied her. She used to do a series of twelve statuesque poses, including the Lady of Spain, Helen of Troy and Diana the Huntress. When she was being Diana, someone would bring on a stuffed greyhound to enhance the illusion.

At the end of Margot's routine, all of the girls would come out and do a military march around her, saluting, while she was draped with a Union Jack and handed a shield, always with one tit hanging out.

After this thrilling finale, we went onstage to reprise our opening number, which went:

THE SAUCY GIRLS OF 1952

There's something here you will enjoy
Saucy Girls, there's something here for every boy
You will find in this sparkling revue a smile, a song, variety, too,
Music and laughter, we have it in store
And when it's all over you will shout for more
So it's goodbye to you

From the Saucy Girls of 1952

No one ever shouted for more.

Apart from the nudes, the other reason we ran for two years was because we changed the name of the show before we returned to a town to make it seem new. The titles included *Up the Girls*, *Evening News* and *THIS IS THE SHOW*, which, from a distance, on a poster looked like *TITS*.

My father had never seen a nude until he visited me backstage at a show in Clapham. He was shattered because he'd brought along a bank manager friend to impress him with his son's show-biz talent. He had thought that maybe he and the bank manager could invest in me. Once he'd seen *Saucy Girls* all that went out of the window. Years later I found out that the bank manager wasn't quite as disappointed by my career choice. On the contrary, he was fascinated by it and couldn't believe I was being paid to be around all those exotic girls.

When word came down that the show was well and truly done, we returned to the markets. Then, out of the blue, we had an offer to take our act to France and Germany to entertain at the military bases. We had heard that if you were reasonably competent you could make a living touring American bases and entertaining mostly drunk, stressed-out soldiers. We seemed to spend a lot of our time dodging things being thrown at us.

We toured for five or six months and ended up stranded in France with no money. The agent who booked us had done the same for eight other acts and assured us that our pay would come. It never did. My mistrust of agents has never left me. So, we were stuck in the middle of France with no money. Matters worsened when I found myself in the middle of a race riot. I had never been exposed to any sort of racism. Certainly I had never come across segregation as was then practised in America. While we were in Bordeaux I found myself sitting with a bloke who fascinated me. He had played with the jazz great Clifford Brown. I was so excited to meet him but I was quickly pulled aside and told to stay away from him because there would be trouble.

Just as I was saying, 'Do me a favour,' I heard a horrible scream at the bottom of the stairs outside. A white bloke's skull had been cracked open – and it all kicked off. The confrontation ended with four people dead.

The act finally folded in 1954. Those days were wild but I was glad they were over.

TIME

I heard it said that it'll save time,
An hour a day.
And what will we do with the hour we save?
Add them together?
And in a week we'll have seven hours,
Our own time to invest.
Time for what?
Time.

By now I was writing every day and starting to like what I was coming up with. I would just vomit it out and try not to judge what I had written until after I'd had a cuppa and a ciggy the next morning.

It feels like Christmas when you open a page and see something good there. It got to the point where I couldn't do anything but write. I gave my pieces to anyone I thought might help me get work.

In terms of originality, my writing didn't seem to be like anything I was reading, and I was inspired by writers like Spike Milligan. I was finding it easier to write funny things, and even though poverty made me miserable, I remained optimistic about my ability. Writing comedy is like working with a safety valve.

I'm sure it always has been since the first jokes. I don't know what the first actual joke was but I suspect it involved cavemen and sabre-tooth tigers. Religion was a favourite theme.

GOD: A SKETCH IDEA

Subject: Good evening.

God: You're welcome, my son.

S: I beg your pardon?

G: You said, 'Good evening,' and I said, 'You're welcome.' I do the best I can.

S: Excuse me – you're God?

G: Bloody right, my son, the Holy Gaffer Himself. What's the matter with you, my son?

S: Nothing, it's just that . . .

G: Spit it out, mate. I can't lig around here indeferably, you know. My eyE is on the flaming sparrow, my son. Do you realise I got to keep my minces peeled on a billion five hundred and thirty-three sparrows? Even they come in a hundred and fifty-odd varieties, that's not to mention all the hippos, badgers, parrots, water voles, et cetera, et cetera, what I created in my infinite wisdom and all. What's on your mind, son?

S: Nothing, it's just that I expected God to be something like . . . well, you know, like the illustrations in the Bible.

G: You expect me to go poncing around with whiskers and a white frock, then? You think I'm a hippie pooftah, mate?

S: No, it's just . . .

G: Only you don't want to get leery, son. I could smite you, if I so chose. I could give you a right smiting, son, plague of bleeding locusts . . . frogs and whatnots . . . In my infinite wisdom I could smite you with leprosy . . . so watch it.

S: No, it's just I imagined God would be . . .

G: More upper class, then? Well, I'm a working-class God, my son, built the bloody world in six days, I did, hand-built and all, put in every star with my own hands, craftsmanship. You don't get that kind of work these days . . . Now, be on your way before the whatnots show up, my son.

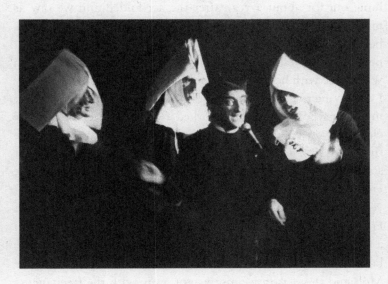

Writing comedy, even before performing it, gave me a great release. The idea that all comics are miserable is bullshit and romanticises the comic's function. All people are miserable, happy and everything in between. I've always known that comedy is what I do, not what I am. That gave me the freedom to take my writing to the outer edges.

Comedy to me is like sport: it releases a lot of emotions – aggression, fury and such. For me it's full-on catharsis.

Unlike my poetry, which I use to synthesise my thoughts, comedy releases all of my emotions. I'd started seeing a bird called Dorothy around this time. God love her, she just wanted to shag and maybe have a bit of a laugh, but I would run all my ideas past her. I didn't care whether she was awake or not, I just needed to direct them at someone. She was one of the Saucy Girls towards the end of our run, and another girl told me Dorothy liked me, even though she thought I looked mad. We hung out for about a year after the act folded and we saw as many films as we could sneak into. We always got in for free because we had a great caper. She would walk up to the ticket person and say she was running late from work and her mum was inside with her ticket. I would arrive not long after and say I was trying to get the keys to our house from either my mum or my sister who was inside. It worked every time, even though the cinemas were empty. We liked weird movies. My favourite at the time was *Monsieur Hulot's Holiday* by Jacques Tati. I'd seen it so many times that I knew every scene by heart. She loved the French seaside resort in it and thought it was dreamy. She was a very horny girl and got off on me jumping her while speaking in French. Her passionate screams could be heard for miles. I got a reputation for being a ladies' man when the fact was she was bonkers. It turned out that her dad was connected with the Mob and the reason we always got away with the free cinema caper and no one told her to stop screaming was because they were petrified.

I THINK

I think therefore I am, I think.
At least I think I am or do I only think I think?
Am I really in this jam?
Because I really think at heart
I put the horse before Descartes.
I am therefore I think if I am
I think I know
That thinking doesn't make it so.
So what do I know, what do I think?
I think I know I need a drink.

I learned from music hall that everyone stole from everyone else and the audience didn't care. Rather, they enjoyed the familiarity.

TIME TAKES TIME

He said, 'It will kill time.'
How strange the notion that time is something to be killed.
How odd the idea that time's not something to be filled
When all we have is time that passes that is not something to be
passed
That is if you have the Time.

Time was briskly passing and at the age of twenty-one, I was finally free to hawk my comedy around without having to worry about the others in our erstwhile act. Even now I wonder how I ever got the nerve but there was no stopping me.

I was well impressed with my ability, and I was starting to find my way.

This was my **time.**

I didn't know that shows had writers. I was beyond naïve. I was convinced they were all Keatons and Chaplins, who pulled the whole thing together themselves. I had an in with a bloke whose sister worked on *The Arthur Haynes Show* and pitched my writing to its producers, not knowing that they already had a writer, and a bloody good one at that, in Johnny Speight. I didn't understand when they said, 'No, we have a writer.' It turned out that they had hired him just as they would a lighting or sound person and that was that.

Around this time I was lucky to meet John Law, who taught me a great deal about writing and set me on the right path. Luck at last.

Dylan Thomas and Brendan Behan were great writers and everyone knew them in the pubs as great writers and they got away with all sorts of behaviour because of their fiery reputations. They knew instinctively how to write. I had a lot less talent but all the willingness to improve. John persuaded me to hone my work and get to the core of what I was about as a writer. He had seen our act in Scotland the year before and we had become friendly. We shared a lot of common interests. We loved American humorists like S. J. Perelman and James Thurber and could quote each other passages of their work. He encouraged me to write comedy I could sell, and would sit me down in his flat, work out the bare bones of an idea with me, then go off for a couple of hours. When he returned he would help me edit all the ideas together. Georgia Brown's brother was the first to buy one of my jokes but John started my career in writing.

Bless him.

He drove Roger Hancock crazy by badgering him to buy one of my pieces. At the time Roger was working on *The Arthur Haynes Show* for George and Alfred Black and eventually bought one of my ideas for a few shillings. It turned out that he had no intention of using it: he just wanted rid of John Law.

But, still, I was up and running, a writer who could sell his own material, even if the means were somewhat suspect.

I went through a long period of ghost-writing for different people, and there were lots of long periods when nothing happened, until suddenly it was coming hard and fast. If only we could see a bit of our future we might do better at what we're doing. Most of my writing was erratic but I was still confident that this was what I should be doing. However, there was a Catch-22: I couldn't join the union but had to be in the union to make it as a writer. It made no sense. I wrote for many great shows and people but I still couldn't join.

I soon got a job writing full-time on a show with a ventriloquist and his dummy called *Educating Archie* – Bruce Forsyth, Benny Hill, the young Julie Andrews and other future stars also appeared on it. At last I was officially a writer, a professional one, even if the union didn't think so. Ronald Wolfe, a real pro, also wrote for the show, and over the two years I worked with him I learned a lot about the mechanics of writing.

Peter Brough didn't do any actual ventriloquism: he just opened his mouth as wide as he could for both parts, with the dummy perched on his knee. He knew that if the show wasn't getting laughs he could spin the dummy's head and get a big laugh. He did this just once in every show, waiting for a failed joke. Then, just before the audience could sigh, he would spin the dummy's head and they would go nuts. It worked every time. I often wondered what those listening to their radios at home thought was going on.

I liked Peter, who was a nice man, but I used to get fed up with the dummy. I found the whole thing bizarre. On the one hand I was writing as a twelve-year-old boy but the dummy looked like a very small adult. Peter was consumed by 'the little fella', as he called him. He would give me presents from him, which worried me no end. I've never met a ventriloquist I liked, other than Peter. Comics often hate them because they get laughs that they themselves would never get away with.

I was making a bit of a living now as a writer, and even though the stuff I was selling wasn't the best I could come up with, I could see a shaft of bright light. I got involved in experimenting with tapes, recording bits of plays with John Law. He was so good at getting me to focus and harness my flights of fancy. I was crashing wherever I could with friends so I did odd jobs to feed myself and give a bit of cash to my 'landlord'.

I set myself exercises in writing for dead people. I would pen stuff that purported to be by a dead writer, weird poems from 'the other side' – anything to keep the fingers moving.

CU P tea and egg on toast.
egg on toast coming up.
did you say egg on toast.
Yes,isn't that what you....
Not egg and toast?
No. You didn't say...
You're offering me egg on toast. You do realise
breads rationed sir. The egg & the toast must
be served separately/as two distinct dishes,which
on two different plates
is the maximum allowed.
I din't know that
I'm telling you ent I? Ministry of Food regulations
sub section 43. You should know subsection 43
by heart mate.
Well I didn't. I'I mean how do you know that unless...
Unless what sir (TAK S OUT PAD & STARTS TO WRITE)
Unless....You're not an Inspector are you
Did I say I was?
 o but....
And did I say I wa n't
You didn't
I did not. Neither way.Did I even infer it?
No but..
So xxx previous to my question you did not think
I was an Inspector from the Ministry of Food.
No I didnt.
(AS HE WRITES) Didn't think.
Didn't think what?
I didn't think you were an inspector from the Minister
of Food.
(WRITING) He stated that he didn't think I was
an Ins ector....
What are you writing?
Just recording what you said. You wouldn't have offer
me egg and toast together on one plate if you'd
suspected that I was what I xxnever said I was.
Look. Do you have to report me.
No. I don't have to report you.
Look can't we straighten this out. If you was to
come back when I've er - when I've got some money
in the till...I could er...
xxxxxxxxxxxxxxxxxxxxxxxxx Don't say it.Don't say
it. I can see you're a decent man trying to
make a living. Just forget anything you said

                    (TEARS UP PAGE (
                              FROM PAD)

Thats very kind of you sir. Could I at least
show my gratitude.
Please. No more. I'll just have two eggs and toast.
Of course. On the house.
You're very kind. Two separate plates mind.
  I got it. Two.

My weapon of mass distraction

THE SLEEP GLEEP

Beware the dreaded nocturnal Gleep
He lurks in the corners of your sleep.
All day he grunges his wanglies tight,
And whirdles skronk till the lovely night.

When your eyElids shudder
And he hears you snore,
Then his toenails mutter and his kneecaps roar
And his eyEballs hum and his teeth all whirr,

And his ears spin clockwise in a three-quarter blur.
Then he spongs his futtocks as he sweevely leaps
And he lunges as he munges
As he gleeps and gleeps.

He will feed on your shadow,
He will suck on your screams,
He will nest in your brain
And infest all your dreams.

But when you awake,
He'll be home snug and tight
Just whirdling his skronk
And awaiting . . . tonight.

At this time writers were in demand and performers were starting to write. John Law was getting work of his own, so had less time to spend with me, and I was writing with other people as well.

It was around this time that Barry Took and I, to our mutual surprise, became each other's main writing partner for almost ten years. We'd met a few years before, in York, when he was doing a stand-up act. I was still with Maurice, Marty and Mitch, and remember seeing him and finding him interesting but, like me and others, he was neither polished nor ready. That drew us together. Barry was open and smart: he asked me for pointers and vice versa. We became friends during that week – I suppose the fact that we were both under sixty bonded us!

Neither of us had much ego. We just wanted to get better and rise above where we were. Very few people under sixty performed on variety bills so we youngsters tended to bundle together: our elders didn't want to give us any ground. Refreshingly, though, writers who were older than us, or established, were great at bringing us into the fold, and smart enough to know that they needed to change with the times. As a result of The Goons, things were changing in a hurry. Since our date in York, Barry had become a writer and was doing well with the radio show *Beyond Our Ken*. Together we wrote a crime serial, which we never sold, but we discovered we had much in common. We were quite similar in many ways: we liked the same music, same authors, we both thought outside the box, and what I lacked in discipline I made up for in creativeness and drive. Mostly we loved to make each other laugh, and often did.

We wrote the last series of *Take It From Here*, after Frank Muir and Denis Norden had left. The producers asked for Barry to take over, as he already had a reputation as a writer, with *Beyond Our Ken*, and he brought me in because he thought we would do well, and we did – bloody well.

I recently found a postcard I wrote but forgot to send him. An unsent Postcard to Barry:

Dear Barry,

Thinking of you, wondering how you are. I'm working well and it's ninety-seven in the shade and another day in paradise ho-hum. I miss you and the occasional fix of reality and it's not too bad if Rumpole of the Bailey's on the telly and I'm playing soccer on Sunday and hanging out with Stanley Dorfman and talking about Barry Lupino and D.M.W and the B & W Minstrels but still . . .

I'm thinking that we might come to London soon for a telly special and if we do and you are about we would love to hang adjacent.

If you've the time, do write and tell us how come you've time to write. Love to you and yours, fond smiles and whiskied affection,

Freedom is the best thing you can offer a friend. We were united by our interests but bonded by our ability as comic writers. We spent most of our time together laughing, not writing, which is a good way to share a workplace with someone.

In terms of writing influences *The Goon Show* is my father and *Take It From Here* is my mum. I was born on the wrong side of the blanket from these two shows. Writing for radio and telly is exciting at first but that soon wears off – with a radio series you eventually run out of scenarios to keep the audience interested. Telly is a bit easier because you can rely more on the physicality of the performers. Great actors can make a script explode. Much of what ended up in my scripts was based on my life and the characters I'd come across. I am intensely religious without having a religion, and I identify with all persecuted minorities: this is reflected in my work.

Writing for me, like most things in my life, is an obsession, a pathological condition that I carry with me, like a badge of dishonour.

The *Round the Horne* Crew

Barry and I found out early that we had a rapport and that our personalities clashed enough to give us a kind of north-south relationship, which we needed to strike off each other. We never defined or even discussed our individual roles, but knew from the beginning what our strengths were. Barry was a great editor and far more disciplined in every way than I was. He was great at getting to the core of an idea and keeping it simple; he was open to any subject and homed in on things that I would often be veering away from, off on one of my many tangents.

We didn't set out to become a team. We said we would work together and see how it went. From the start, I hoped we would be a team because I saw in him many things I couldn't do but needed to, and I think he liked my free spirit and outlandish, surreal sense of humour. Once we got going we wouldn't know or care who had come up with an idea. It would vary from day to day and sometimes by the minute. There were times when I would produce a marvellous plot and Barry would decorate it – I the architect and he the interior designer – and the next day it would be the other way around. This kind of elasticity worked for us.

By nature I am a collaborator. Many prefer to write alone, but the collaboration between my mum and dad that resulted in me comes out in my writing: the masculine and a good dose of feminine, too. Writers who work in teams are like most marriages: they are reasonably faithful to one another for as long as the marriage lasts. I still think of Barry when putting a team together, no matter what the project, and, like Spike, he'll always top my list.

There used to be a live Wednesday-afternoon show on telly called *Fancy Free*, produced by Anna Lett, who had become a chum. One day, Anna called and asked Barry and me to come down and do something. We turned up and sang a song. It became a habit – we'd sing, do a sketch, whatever, never thinking anyone was watching. Even Morris, Marty and Mitch did a turn before we folded. Expectations were low. Barry and I called it our Wednesday-afternoon club. Eventually, we thought it couldn't hurt to try out one of our new sketches, and it was fun, which was not a word I would've used for any of my stage performances.

Once I'd done a few telly things, John Law told me I should start doing regular stage work. He and I cobbled together an act, which I did at the Nuffield Centre. I kept it short and physical, and the crowd really seemed to like me. John knew a big-time comedy agent and encouraged him to catch me on *Fancy Free* but also to come and see me live on stage at this gig. Soon he was calling me to say I should stay by the phone because the agent had done both and would be calling.

Sure enough, two days later the guy rang me up and said, 'Can I be frank?'

I was a bit nervous. 'You're free to be anyone you like.' That was followed by a long silence.

Then he said, 'You don't have it. You're not a comic. You may be a good writer, but you should stick to what you know.'

I lost my bottle and immediately tried to get out of all appearances, especially Anna's *Fancy Free*. When I told John, he thought I was having him on, that I saw more money in writing and had deliberately put the agent off. If only.

That agent could've been one of the key figures in my career and life.

It wasn't true that I couldn't make people laugh. I could. I might not have been the best, but I was far from the worst. I didn't perform for a long while after that, but because the writing was going well, I was in a strong enough place to bury the knockback. I often wonder how many other young performers with potential that agent put off. It would've been just as easy to say something encouraging and left it at that.

As Fate would have it, like Robert Redford before me, my looks would open the door later to a performing career. To this day, I am weary of agents and critics: I see that, through their lack of understanding, millions of people are denied great works. A decent review can be essential in bringing new drama, music and books to us all. If Shakespeare were around today they would have him writing for telly. Bernard Shaw would be hosting a Sunday-night talk show and Duke Ellington would be writing jingles for adverts.

A graphologist can tell something about me from the way I write my name, even more from the way I construct a sentence, but the majority of critics couldn't find humour if it jumped out of their soup. I once worked on a show as script editor and the critic Maurice Richardson was invited to write a script. He sent it to me, and as editor I had to turn it down because it was bloody awful. I sent it back with a note saying it didn't work for that particular show, but keep going, and other nice stuff. After that he never reviewed anything I wrote or performed.

About six months after my setback with that agent, John Law was still telling me I had it in me to perform. He convinced one of my heroes, Michael Bentine of the Goons, to use me in a TV show, which he was doing for ATV. Michael had no clue who the hell I was and had no reason to. Many years before I met him I did an impression of him when Maurice, Marty and Mitch were trying to fill gaps between appearances of the Saucy Girls. We met at a coffee bar, and the very first thing he said to me was 'Can you do a Scottish accent?'

I said I could. I had no idea whether I could or not. When someone is interviewing you for a job and asks if you can do this or that, say, 'Yes,' and worry about it after you get the job. I got hired to do three shows for ATV. I couldn't believe it. Lew Grade, who was as big a mogul as any, told Michael I was very good and should be featured. The shows never went to air.

Not long after, John Law wrote a series called *Three Tough Guys*. Lew Grade watched me through the pilot and didn't recognise me. Long cigars, short memory! That show wasn't picked up either. A year later I bumped into Bentine again. 'Oh, that face, this face, I have to do something with this face.' He insisted I would be his co-star in his brand-new series. I thought this was it: I was really going to be an actor this time. I was so excited. Even the idea of the show, based on a parody of *Faust*, was thrilling.

I didn't hear from Michael for a week, and when I finally got hold of him, he had forgotten me.

Back to writing I went. I wrote for anyone who would have me. One thing that really kept me going was writing some sketches on spec for Alfred Marks and others. Alfred was doing a telly series and took time out of his busy schedule to tell me that, although they couldn't use the material I'd submitted, I should keep going: he thought I was going to make it. Which was hard to believe: I was getting rejection slips from all over the shop and hadn't sold anything in months. I was about to throw in the towel and go back to working in the markets.

His letter, written elegantly on blue paper, just telling me to keep going, meant the world to me. His encouragement was worth more than money. Money comes and goes but encouragement stays.

It wasn't long before Barry and I were asked to join the writing team of a hit show called *The Army Game*, just what we needed. I soon learned that writing for a comedy series was a craft. I have read plays by people who had never written anything before and enjoyed them and the same goes for novels, but I have never laughed at a good comedy script by someone who has never written one before. It has less to do with talent and more to do with expertise. You need an aware eyE and an aware ear, and there is a skill in making people laugh. Tapping into the shared sense of humour of a nation became my goal. Some of the best writers of radio and television were starting to cross my path. Denis Norden, Frank Muir, Johnny Speight, Ronald Wolfe and Alan Simpson were all established, but before long Barry, John Law and I had joined the ranks.

Soon Barry and I went from being part of *The Army Game*'s team and branched off as a writing partnership. We became Feldman and Took after we'd been Took and Feldman, not that it ever mattered because no one knew which was which anyway. We were both represented by Kenneth Ewing, whom I retained as my agent through a lot of years and a lot of changes. *The Army Game* was fun and we found our feet. Someone at the network recognised this and offered us our own show. After many horrible title ideas, it was called *Bootsie and Snudge*. And I became financially stable for the first time in my life at the ripe old age of thirty.

I was also writing for a show called *Comedy Playhouse*. This was a testing ground for pilots, and if you got lucky with your script you'd get a series. I pitched many scripts and the one that landed was *The Walrus and the Carpenter*, which was well received, but not picked up as a series. It was inspired by people from the days and nights I spent in parks. The character Luther Flannery was based partly on my grandfather, a full-on Russian Jew with a big beard and as traditional as you could find. When the world was preoccupied with youth and the Liverpool music scene, Barry and I wrote about two old men in the 'Anteroom of Death', Flannery and Quilt, played by Hugh Griffith and Felix Aylmer. One had travelled the world and learned nothing while the other had gone nowhere and knew it all. The elderly do sit around graveyards, and when one dies they all move up the bench. Old men, in particular, are like children: both groups do daft things, mostly without intent, and we can laugh at them. Barry is six years older than me, and I've always hung out with older people because I learn so much from them.

I never knew from one day to the next what show I was writing on. I was hopeless at saying no, and became swamped with work. Luckily, Barry was my anchor. I was starting to feel depressed, was always tired and irritable through lack of sleep. Now I think of that time as BL 'Before Lauretta': I had been flailing, and the missing link I had yearned for was soon to arrive in my life. Never soon enough!

A happy crew

Me and Barry, Barry and I.

LAST NIGHT
(POEM FOR LAURETTA)

You called my name, reached me and touched me in my sleep
Where no one ever touched me
Where no one ever reached me
Where no one ever called me
Somewhere so deep inside me
In what we call a soul.

I held you gently, silently venerating your sweet breath
So close upon my pillow, so dear unto my senses.
Somehow you heard my spirit
Somewhere so deep inside you, and smiled in answering love.

There is nowhere I can go
Where you are not,
Nothing I can feel
But you are part.
You the light, me the candlestick,
To warn the night
In what we call my heart.

On the night of 12 April 1958 I met Lauretta, the love of my life. We were at a jazz club called El Toro on London's Finchley Road. It was late and I had been drunk for what seemed days. I was making a fool of myself. According to Lauretta, a mutual chum had told her we should meet each other. All I remember is that I heard this wonderful husky female voice talking behind me, and as I turned, I felt like I had been struck by a bolt of lightning when I saw the woman who owned the voice. I said something like, 'What a great voice you have.'

'You have one, too, and it's too bloody loud,' she said. We ended up chatting for hours about everything we loved. That night I really felt my life was on the up.

Chatting with a real bird, and having a few bob in my pocket, from being a paid professional writer, was nice. I was carrying my trumpet case and she noticed it and asked whether I played it or if it was something to hide behind. I admitted the case was empty because I'd sold the trumpet to a bloke who'd had his stolen but didn't need the case. Really, like the booze, it served as a buffer.

At the time, Lauretta Sullivan was working in a kids' talent agency as a secretary, and in her time off was dedicated to her dance lessons. I couldn't think of anything but her, and held onto her telephone number for hours. The next day I called her at work and told her we must meet as soon as she had the time. I couldn't breathe and my heart was racing. I'd never felt anything like that before.

That same day we met outside her office and she looked even more beautiful than she had the night before. We sat together on a wall opposite her agency and I told her how I was feeling, and she said, 'Well, we'd better get you a drink, then.' On the way to the pub she reached for my hand and said she felt the same. Little did I know she had gone home in the wee small hours, woken her mum and told her she had met the man she would spend the rest of her life with. Heaven on earth! I couldn't believe it.

We moved in together right away, and although our families objected, we couldn't have cared less. My mother, in particular, was very disapproving, primarily because Lauretta wasn't Jewish. I told Lauretta about my mother's thoughts and she said, 'Well, Mart, she has her family and now you have your own.' Our dads were both cool about it, even though her dad was a butcher: I was a vegetarian, which he thought was a crazy Jewish thing. My dad took one look at Lauretta and glanced at me as if to say, 'Go on, my son.' He never figured out how I'd pulled it off. Unlike my mum, he said not one negative thing about her. I thought they would just be happy I'd found someone. My relationship with my mum never really recovered, no matter how we tried.

Lauretta couldn't have come into my life at a better time. Work with Barry was getting really busy, and as much as I was happy to be collaborating on so many different projects, the pressure was mounting and I needed something to take my head away from it. Lauretta became my biggest supporter, always good at making me realise I needed to enjoy life more and not to take everything so full on. Perfectionism can wear anybody out but she would constantly remind me that there is life outside work.

Our flat quickly became the focus of many a great gathering. I hated going out because I was working so hard, but Lauretta always managed to have the right people over who relaxed me. She had a very different group of friends from mine. I had narrowed mine down to one or two writers. She hung out with dancers and performers, a wild and varied bunch, creative types who almost spoke their own language. Nothing ever fazes Lauretta and she's a great judge of character: there's safety in her numbers. She and I found a shared fugue state and couldn't have been happier.

One morning, I woke up and thought I was having a stroke. I was trying to hold my teacup but couldn't. I'd been having that sensation for a while. I told Lauretta I wasn't feeling well and we went to the hospital where I was put through a battery of tests. Eventually I was diagnosed with a severely overactive thyroid gland. It was recommended I have surgery immediately. Barry and I had been working very intensively and were in the middle of a series so I had to hold off treatment for a few months. I was very depressed, had lost weight and found it very difficult to sleep, eat or think straight. One moment I was floating with happiness and the next I was in miserable pain. I put up with it for as long as I could, but finally went into hospital and my dodgy thyroid came out. They removed 90 per cent of it, and I was home within five days. They wanted to keep me longer but I had to go back to work: we were hacking out scripts for *Bootsie and Snudge*, among other jobs, and even though the surgeon had cut me from ear to ear I was feeling much better. I was prescribed medication to replace my missing gland.

Not long after I got home, Lauretta noticed that my eyEs were a strange colour and were beginning to bulge. One had been showing signs of laziness and was now getting worse. Years before this, when I was around twelve, I'd had a boating accident. I'd taken a very small boat out at night on the Norfolk Broads and, for no reason at all, decided to stand up. I lost my balance, fell into the water and couldn't find my way back to the surface. I think I banged my head and lost myself for a bit. I was eventually rescued by a younger Boy Scout, which was rather humiliating, but I was extremely grateful! What does a Jew know about sailing? More to the point, why was I even in the boat?

I think I always had a lazy or, as I prefer to call it, noncompetitive eyE. Anyway, after the surgery, Lauretta noticed that the eyE was straying so I told her it had done so ever since my boat accident.

Other people noticed it when I was tired. She thought it was worsening.

If I hadn't been injured boxing for the Jewish Lads Brigade, I wouldn't have this plonker of a nose. If I'd been a better cricketer I could have caught the ball that left a dent on my forehead. If I hadn't been on a boat standing up, like a fool, or hadn't been attacked by a kid with a pencil at school, or hadn't been writing thirty-nine television shows a year, plus twenty-six radio shows, my eyEs might not have popped out, regardless of the thyroid condition.

Still, despite it all, I was starting to like the cut of my jib, and with a few bob coming in, and the most beautiful bird in the world by my side, it could've been worse.

The first couple of years we were together, I used to get fed up with people staring at my bird, but after my eyEs made their obtrusive debut those people weren't always staring at *her*, and Lauretta would get well pissed off. She became quite vocal in my defence, a trend that continued, for which I am most grateful.

eYE

Time wearies the grieving bone
Bares the illusion that flares the poet's eyE.
The terror of time did bare the grieving bone
Aches for inconsequence where once illusion
Flared even the ever dodgy poet's eyE.

A week after the operation, I returned to the hospital and was told by a doctor that I was having a negative reaction to the medication and that the only way to fix the protruding eyE was to remove it, tighten the ligaments, then put it back in.

I was petrified.

When I asked Lauretta what she thought I should do, she said, 'It's your eyE, Mart.' When I asked her if she would find me grotesque if I didn't change it, she said, 'I'll just look at the other eyE, and at least you have a nice cock!'

Words of comfort from the one I loved most.

Barry, ever the gentleman, told me he hadn't even noticed the eyE and thought I was making too much of it. He said it was just stress from overworking, which, he added, was about to make his eyEs invert.

At this time Lauretta became more involved in my career, much to my relief. She made sure I always had one day off every week, got out of the house and went to see a football game or a show. We even planned and went on holidays overseas. For my birthday she bought me a beautiful wallet, with a picture of my hero Buster Keaton inside. I always have it with me to remind me that even when you have talent and work your arse off it can be taken away from you, leaving you with nothing.

We have always been extremely protective of each other and get more so as we age. I remember once being at a peace march, and before I knew it I was surrounded by coppers. I thought, Do I spend a night in jail or fight for what I'm here for? I ducked under the cordon and sneaked home. When a journalist clocked me leaving and later asked me to comment, Lauretta interrupted and said that I was rushing home to take care of her because she had been ill. That sort of thing went on all the time and we never really wanted to leave our house or each other for anything. Let them bomb all around us. I've always lived in the now, an ever-changing now. I've always been the type who does whatever seems to make sense at the time. A pragmatic approach to a career, maybe, but Lauretta broadened my horizons and made me see things in the longer term, which soon had a huge effect on my career. It turned out that saying, 'No,' can actually do wonders for a career.

That Christmas was a landmark time for Lauretta and me. Our families were pressuring us to get married because we lived together. My mother became even more vitriolic and made sure that everyone knew she didn't approve of Lauretta. So, we got a marriage licence, and in the early hours of 14 January I ducked out of work and we got married at the Caxton Hall register office. It was a reaction to an ultimatum my mother had issued when she heard I was going to Lauretta's family home for Christmas.

She told me never to come back to her house unless I was no longer seeing Lauretta. That did my head in. I thought, We'll get married now and in time they'll come around . . . or not.

Wife!

I met Spike Milligan at a party and he told me that Lauretta was the most beautiful woman he had ever seen and because he was taller than me he was going to run away with her and I would never catch him. We immediately hit it off, and he is one of my favourite people. I'm not alone in thinking that Spike is indeed a genius, a true original who never fails to surprise with his vast physical and mental prowess.

I told him about my family problem and he recommended a psychiatrist. I thought things must be really bad if he was telling me to see one, but I went ahead anyway. At my first visit, the shrink asked, 'What is fucking you up, Mart?'

I told him about my family's reaction to my girl and the stress I was under from that and my work schedule. I was making little money and was newly married – I'd even had to borrow cash to pay for a night in a hotel room for our honeymoon. I wanted to take care of my old lady, but funds were tight. He listened, didn't say much, then told me I should come back and see him every week. The next day, I received his bill.

Round the Horne was the show for which Barry and I would soon become recognised. It featured many great talents, primarily the Kenneths, Williams and Horne. It was like a front-row seat to the best acting class. Although Kenneth Horne got a lot of funny lines, he was the best straight man I had ever seen, gentle, with a big heart, very still and confident but not cocky. The other Ken was wild, so much fun to work with – he knew no limits. Hugh Paddick, too, was a wonder.

Julian and Sandy was another show we did around this time. The lead characters, played by Hugh Paddick and Kenneth Williams, were gay before gay was allowed and we really let rip with them. The show was broadcast live on the radio from a theatre. There was a great sense of community within our group.

The team effort was strong and everyone liked each other. Kenneth Horne was in it, too, and made a relaxed environment: he would always take care of everyone as the most experienced among us. The audiences lined up around the building and down the street hoping to get tickets. The actors would be set up with their microphones in front of the theatre stage while a full orchestra accompanied them. Barry and I sat in the front row with our backs to the crowd and, at times, it felt like a Beatles show. It was hugely influential, a true link between the Goons and the Pythons. Barry and I struck a chord with it and it remains among our best work.

After that show finished Lauretta and I took a holiday, our proper honeymoon. It was my first actual holiday since I was a kid. Our work and social lives were hectic beyond belief so just to lie on a beach and not think about anything that was going on at home was bliss. Holidays soon became an essential part of our lives and Lauretta would announce, as soon as she saw a break coming, where we'd be spending our down time: Antibes and Elba were our favourites.

We met all sorts of interesting characters on those trips. Often our dear friends Anne and Ted Levy came with us. Ted was a steady chap and a very gifted architect. He was also a friend of Peter Sellers and was working on a house for him when Sellers's marriage to Anne Howe was going south. Anne and Lauretta became very close. Hearing them cackle together was a treat.

Julian and Sandy

F/X	**CHIMES DOORBELL. DOOR OPENS.**
JULIAN (Hugh Paddick)	Hello. We're from Rentachap. I'm Julian and this is my friend, Sandy.
SANDY (Kenneth Williams)	We've come to do for you — (*whispers*) That's never Kenneth Horne.
JULIAN	(*whispers*) It is — it is.
SANDY	(*whispers*) He's quite old isn't he? I wonder if they're his own teeth?
JULIAN	(*whispers*) Ask him.
SANDY	(*whispers*) I don't like to.
Kenneth Horne	Look, have you just popped round to make comments on my personal appearance or are you going to do the housework?
JULIAN	We're seven-and-six an hour you know. Did Miss Brahms at the agency warn you?
Kenneth Horne	Yes, we agreed terms. Quick come in before the neighbours see you. Now, are you experienced in this sort of work?
JULIAN	Well, not exactly — you see we're filling in between engagements — we do commercials mostly — you may have seen us on the telly — you know that ad where she's got it only no-one'll tell her — only someone does, then she has a bath —
Kenneth Horne	Yes.
JULIAN	Well — she gets me dragged up as a rugby full back.
SANDY	And I'm in the one where I'm alone in a room with this beautiful girl and we put out the lights and test chocolates.
Kenneth Horne	I'm not altogether surprised. Now, let me show you what I want doing. This is the living room.
SANDY	Oh ducky, it's pure Rattigan — with a touch of Messel round the Dado.
Kenneth Horne	And through here's the kitchen.
JULIAN	It's a bit Arnold Wesker isn't it? No, I'm afraid not. Kitchen sink isn't us — heartette — we're more drawing-room comedy — or bedroom farce.
Kenneth Horne	Well, do the best you can — here's the dishcloths.
SANDY	Ugh! Green and yellow — we can't be doing with that.
Kenneth Horne	What's the matter with green and yellow dishcloths?

JULIAN	Well see for yourself treash. We're wearing blue — doesn't match at all. No, anyway, we couldn't wash up in here — all the dishes are dirty —
Kenneth Horne	Well, I'm sorry, I'd have washed them up if I'd known.
SANDY	It's the grease, you see — it turns his stomach over. Some people can cope, darling heart, but whenever Julian is confronted with greasy dishes, he bursts into tears.
Kenneth Horne	Well, I wouldn't want to upset him. Perhaps you'd better start on the living room.
JULIAN	Oh yes, that's much more us — Oh look Sandy — a parquet floor — bona! I wish I'd known — I'd have brought me tap-shoes.
Kenneth Horne	If it's all the same to you — I don't want you to dance on it. I want you to polish it.
JULIAN	I'm not going down on my hands and knees — I shall bag me Levis.
Kenneth Horne	Well, dust something then — there, the piano . . .
SANDY	Oh, a piano, heartette.
PIANO	ARPEGGIO
	PIANO PLAYS ACCOMPANIMENT (VERY DATED) TO 'AIN'T SHE SWEET'
	JULIAN AND SANDY SING — WITH APPROPRIATE VO-DE-O-DO's
Kenneth Horne	Stop it, stop it —
	PIANO GOES INTO STOP CHORUS
F/X	TAP DANCING ON WOODEN SURFACE
Kenneth Horne	Stop dancing on my piano. Oi! Bojangles!
	(music stops abruptly)
F/X	CLANG OF PIANO LID BEING SLAMMED DOWN
JULIAN	Well really — that's a nice way to treat an artiste I must say! Bring us here under false pretences — treat us like drudges . . .
SANDY	Don't Julian, don't get yourself worked up. If you frown you'll get crow's feet.
JULIAN	*(hysterically)* I don't care. It's too much — it's all too much. We haven't been put on this earth to wash his dirty dishes and scrape his porridge saucepans. If we wanted to be unskilled labourers we could be working for Joan Littlewood. I'm not staying in this house another minute. Come on, Sandy — good day, Mr Horne — good day.
F/X	DOOR SLAMS. DOORBELL RINGS. DOOR OPENS AGAIN.
Kenneth Horne	Oh it's you again. What is it?
JULIAN	We just wanted to know — what time do you want us tomorrow?
ORCHESTRA	PAY OFF MUSIC
	(applause)

In order to write you have to live or, at least, step outside your comfort zone. A lot of characters' names belonged to real people I bumped into or met on a holiday. I would come home with pockets full of napkins with their dialogue recorded and laugh when Barry asked how I'd come up with such outrageous names.

The late fifties and early sixties were fascinating times to be in some of the exotic locations Lauretta and I visited. We met hustlers and religious people and could never really tell them apart. Everyone in Morocco offered us cannabis and sex. Before our generation started holidaying there, British businessmen made it their Las Vegas and travelled to Morocco for sex and drugs. When Lauretta and I were offered sex while we were sitting or walking along together, I would always ask what exactly they would do, much to my old lady's horror.

On the strength of *Round the Horne* I was getting offers of work from radio, telly and beyond. Barry and I would find ourselves writing our show and running off in opposite directions only to return later to finish off our ideas. Everyone wanted to work with Barry, but he was really good at saying no to other things in order to focus on what he liked doing best. It took me a while to emulate his astute behaviour. I was trying to please everyone, convinced that it would all go away as fast as it had arrived.

David Frost had become a big fan of *Round the Horne* and asked if I would help him produce and script edit his new show, to be called *The Frost Report*. At my already advanced age I was on the verge of becoming a household name. The first order I gave as co-producer was for everyone to go on holiday.

Two of the performers, John Cleese and Graham Chapman, were writing a film for Frost and had rented a huge villa on Ibiza for a few months to get some writing done. Lauretta, Tim Brooke-Taylor, who was also to be on the show, his missus and I invited ourselves to join them. (A working holiday!) When I got there I realised that Barry and I had influenced the work of this newer group of comedy writers: they quoted our stuff. I was chuffed and made it my priority to take care of them. As the show's editor I flexed that muscle.

That holiday was a life-changer for some of us. John had found love with Connie Booth, and Graham met the love of his life there. It set the tone for what was to be a milestone in my life and career.

People have asked me what makes David Frost a good producer and I like to say he's good because he says he is! He had a knack for pulling the right people together. I worked on *The Frost Report* for a year and a half. At the time, the bar at the BBC was full of great writers, young and old alike. Tim Brooke-Taylor

Lauretta and Graham

John and Lauretta

Graham and me

With Tim

With Graham

was one of them. Fresh-faced and innocent, but more than willing to do anything asked of him, he was a very calm person to be around.

Our offices on Crawford Street became the place for writers to be. Cleese and Chapman, David Nobbs, Keith Waterhouse, Michael Palin, Terry Jones, Eric Idle, Barry Cryer, Barry Took and I: what a bunch. Once we were all set up with our typewriters and accoutrements, it was like being in the eyE of the hurricane. Other writers and performers would drop by too. Peter Cook had a great club, which he named the Establishment, and we would all be there when we weren't working and would write sketches and jokes for others to perform, like the great Frankie Howerd, who held court at Peter's place. Frankie was the guv when it came to performing: you could put any words into his mouth and he'd make them funny. All of the writers would pitch him stuff and watch him deliver it live.

The comic Lenny Bruce performed there and we got to know him a bit. It was great to see him work.

Peter had been involved with a show called *Beyond the Fringe*, which featured Alan Bennett, Jonathan Miller, Dudley Moore

and himself. Dudley had a little trio and would play his piano at the Establishment. Quality music and comedy under the same roof: it was very inspiring to be around those great talents.

It's hard to remember who worked on what: it was an extremely fertile period for young writers, who were all hellbent on getting into telly. Alan and Jonathan went on to become huge figures in English culture.

I talk a lot about influential writers and performers but without them we would have no compass and they still challenge us to be better.

I remember meeting Eric Idle, although we got to know each other better later. Like Dudley, he impressed me as someone who could do it all.

The Frost Report was an overnight sensation. An old sketch that I'd written with John Law, based on the class system and all its lunacy, became popular, featuring John Cleese as an upper-class man, Ronnie Barker representing the middle class, and Ronnie Corbett the lower class:

Upper Class: *I look down on him because I am upper class.*
Middle Class: *I look up to him because he is upper class. But I look down on him because he is lower class. I'm middle class.*
Lower Class: *I know my place.*

After it had aired you could hear people in pubs and cafés doing their own interpretations of it. I knew right away that this was a really good entry for me into telly and people's homes. People still quote it to me – 'I know my place.' We had fun writing it, but when we saw the boys doing it we were thrilled beyond belief.

It was around this time that I started feeling the urge to perform again. It was exhilarating to be in the company of those great performers and they inspired me like nobody since Danny Kaye.

I learned a lot from that show and, although I couldn't do what David did, I was starting to feel I could find my way around a show of my own.

The great thing about being established at that level was I could get tickets to see Chelsea play. I would drag a friend along with me and we'd roar our hearts out from the stands for ninety minutes. It was the greatest time to be in England. Our comedy was unique, as was our music. London was well and truly swinging and we had the coppers to enjoy it.

Lauretta and I would go to all the clubs and restaurants and see the best shows, and there was plenty to enjoy. We saw all of my jazz heroes and some pretty great pop shows too. We went to see Ravi Shankar at the Albert Hall and the place was full of famous people: the Beatles and Peter Sellers were in the front row.

Much to my surprise, Lauretta and I were seated next to them and some of them knew who I was, which was nice. I had to leave about twenty minutes into the performance because Lauretta sent me into convulsions of laughter by asking rather loudly, 'Are they still tuning up?'

Barry and I were now being invited to see and take part in other shows and gatherings. We even got to stop by at a Beatles session while they were recording at Abbey Road Studios. I was excited because this was where the Goons had recorded, with the Beatles' producer, George Martin.

A couple of years later Lauretta and I were invited to a Beatles recording that was to be a live broadcast. The Beatles were now dressing with more colour and flair, but most photos and telly were still in black-and-white. We would see them at parties with the Rolling Stones and Keith Moon of the Who and they looked like a circus act. The song they were performing was 'All You Need Is Love' and I remember thinking I wanted to join the circus as soon as possible. I still dressed as a professional writer did at the time, a suit and tie, similar to what the Beatles had worn when they started, and the idea of not wearing a tie or shoes and letting my hair grow seemed the right way to go. A lot of drugs were doing the rounds, which didn't interest me so much, but the overall feeling was one of togetherness: we were working with our talents and clout to make things a bit better in the world.

I remember trying to tell George Harrison that I was feeling a kind of rebirth and he stood right in front of me, very close, with wild eyEs, laughing and saying, 'Mantra Man,' over and over. I didn't think he should be the driver for our mission but he was awfully sweet. Everyone knew that John was the Beatles' governor. He had it all, knew it and relished it.

We didn't limit our writing to the office. Most great comedy is created in real places, and home is no exception. John Cleese and I had very different interests and background, but we still got along very well: we just reached for different shelves! At Lauretta's and my flat, we came up with a lot of great ideas for sketches, as we drank and I forced my jazz records on him. *The Four Yorkshiremen* sketch was born in the kitchen. It's still one of my favourites.

It started with me poking fun at John, which I did whenever he complained about something. Rain? Let me tell you about rain, my son. Tired? We were too poor to be tired. Bloody luxury is sleep, lad. We knew we were on to something good right away. We would try to outdo each other and could hear Lauretta and Anne laughing in the next room. Once Graham and Tim got on board there was no stopping us. Tim in particular wrote some great stuff.

Most people think it was a *Monty Python* sketch – in fact, we wrote it for *At Last the 1948 Show* – which I feel is a compliment because they did it so well. It didn't matter who came up with what as long as the laughs were there. Ian Fordyce was our director and he pretty much ran the show. He was the glue and kept everyone on top of their game.

Tim and I became really close friends after the Ibiza jaunt. The holiday helped immensely because I was feeling quite insecure:

the others were great performers but they were also flatmates and had gone to college together. I was the odd man out.

We needed a girl for the show and people were all trying to think of who would be the right bird for us. There were auditions but it was decided we should find someone new. I decided to take the college boys to one of my old haunts to see some birds I felt could use a break. Maybe one of the Saucy Girls. We went to a club but it was only when the girls started to straddle the boys that we figured out they were proper 'working girls'.

Elsewhere, the lovely Aimi MacDonald had just started working in cabaret and when we saw her do her routine we all knew she was the bird for us. A great wee lass too. She had just come back from America and had great stories. She'd been a backing dancer for Elvis before returning to England.

Lauretta had been under a lot of pressure prior to the Ibiza trip because her dear old mum was very ill. We'd been spending as much time with her as we could. When we returned her mum took a drastic turn for the worse.

Not long after we got back, I had a call from John Cleese asking me to join him on a new show with Tim and Graham, David Frost producing. I said I thought it would be a great show but was feeling overwhelmed by the work I already had. I was still working on several other shows at the time.

When Tim called, I realised they wanted me as a performer. I'd thought John had meant I was needed as a writer but in fact the four of us would be writing and acting. I was shocked and thrilled. I thought I'd do it as a giggle and return to writing, like I had before. When I told Lauretta and her mum, they had conflicting views, but both were supportive. Lauretta's mum said I was funnier than everyone else and she couldn't understand why I wasn't acting already. Little did she know.

I told her she didn't have to be nice: she was dying and could speak freely! Lauretta told me I should think about it: she wanted to remain married to a writer, but thought it possible that we could keep the acting low-profile. Graham and Tim knew I was ambivalent about it but fought hard for me to do it.

We shot the pilot on the same day as my mother-in-law's funeral. It turned into a series and continued for a second season. After I'd accepted the job, I found out that Frost wasn't happy about me joining the show but had been strong-armed into it by John and Graham. Tim told me that Frost had said my 'grotesque looks' would sink the show. He was sure that my 'strange eyEs would turn people off'. Apparently John told him it was the four of us or none.

To this day I am in debt to those men and would jump if any of them needed help.

I understand Frost's concern and wasn't surprised by it. He hadn't recognised that many great comic actors have been unusual-looking – Chaplin too small, Cleese too tall . . . We prevailed against the opposition and went full steam ahead.

The writing was very strong and Cleese developed a fondness for me playing annoying characters, pesky little men with inappropriate languages. We spent too long trying to come up with a title for the show. Trevor Nunn claimed he came up with it but I cracked it with *At Last the 1948 Show*. It was as daft as *The Saucy Girls* or any of the acts I'd come across from Margate onwards. They all loved it and when I told them it meant nothing they liked it all the more.

Suddenly the show was out there and I was doing lots of press. After the second show aired, my long-suffering agent called me to say that the BBC had offered me my own show. I was convinced that Lauretta had had something to do with it or that they were winding me up, but it was true: they wanted me to do my own show. *At Last the 1948 Show* was the show that made me into an overnight something. People recognised me

and I liked it. More often than not, they were nice. The most common remark they made was 'Aren't you the funny bloke with the eyEs from the telly?'

I usually replied, 'No, I'm the tall, good-looking one.'

John and Graham had been talking about their own show before *1948* aired. Tim, too, was being asked. We all knew that we had to have something on the back-burner because shows were often cancelled, and many people never returned afterwards. We hadn't thought *1948* would be picked up because most of it was too weird in comparison with what was on telly at that time.

We were hired to make six thirty-minute shows all in sketch form and all to feature me in some way. Apart from those constraints, the BBC left us alone to cavort and come up with whatever we wanted.

We thought we would face a barrage of silly suggestions, like adding fake applause or canned laughter. The very idea is enough to send me even further around the bend. The BBC's Tom Sloan and our producer Dennis kept at bay anybody who had opinions about production. Canned laughter is absurd: a group of people had laughed at one thing and then it's applied to another? Some of those laughing people are probably dead but now they're laughing at my show? Not on my watch!

Our writers and cast were the best that were around. John Cleese and Graham Chapman joined Barry and me in the writing department, with Michael Palin and Terry Jones, who were two great new writers with fantastic ideas. Tim Brooke-Taylor and John Junkin joined us behind and in front of the camera. It was a dream team.

We really were left to do what we wanted and I even got to throw in contributions from my old friend John Law, Denis Norden and Frank Muir – I'd looked up to them all.

The Loneliness of a Long Distance Golfer would be my favourite sketch, if I had to pick one, but I haven't seen many. The very thought of sitting through one scene with me in it makes me quiver. Lauretta and my agent Kenneth Ewing sat with me in our house to watch the first episode when it was first broadcast and I spent most of the time in the toilet. Lauretta's favourite sketch, *The Lightning Coach*, which featured the line 'Wait for me' was a hit with all the young kids, who yelled at me whenever I was out and about. Some baked pies for me or knitted scarves, and I was happy to take all I was given – many well-known performers were offered sex but my public seemed to look on me as a family member!

Before we could enjoy that *1948* show, I became consumed with doing my own show. I wanted to do as much silent stuff as I could get away with, putting my own twist on it, but I needed the best writers. Barry was obviously my first choice, but I wanted Michael Palin and Terry Jones, too. I even hoped that John Cleese and Graham Chapman would lend a hand – after all, I'd do anything they asked in their ventures. It turned out that Graham and John were about to embark on one of the finest comic journeys ever, to be called *Monty Python's Flying Circus*. When I think about that show's origins I feel proud that we all worked together. With our combined talents we were all destined to cross paths again.

John remains low-key about giving me my big break but I will always be grateful for his support. He has one of the best comedy minds Britain has ever produced. I was quite jealous that I wasn't his Spanish waiter in *Fawlty Towers*. I was never asked but would have loved a juicy role like that alongside him.

The title of my show was *Marty*, but more than ever I felt it needed to be a team effort. I was lucky enough to have Tim Brooke-Taylor, John Junkin, Mary Miller and Roland MacLeod as the cast. Roland and John were trained actors, and I had known John for quite some time so I was delighted to have him opposite me as a straight man. Acting was really fun and I couldn't get enough of it.

I had a small role in a film Spike wrote and Dick Lester directed. It was called *The Bed Sitting Room*, a nutty script Spike had conceived as a play years earlier. When he asked if I would do it I thought he meant as a play and was surprised but thrilled for him that it was a film. I played a male nurse while Dudley Moore and Peter Cook played coppers.

Marty broke rules and records in terms of its high budget. Before I agreed to do it I insisted that the budget would cover filmed segments, like *The Loneliness of the Long Distance Golfer*. (Everyone who got a show after this asked for the same. Some were successful and I think it improved the overall quality of shows at the time. When you ask for quality in a show in terms of budget, it generally means you won't make any money from it.) One of my favourite days shooting on *Marty* involved *Long Distance Golfer*. We were filming on location when I bumped into a couple of my homeless pals from the old days of Soho and the park. We had a smoke and carried on like we were all in the same hole we had been in years before. I tried to have them come in as extras but they were too nutty to handle showing up.

The show was well liked by most and received a bunch of awards although, as I said earlier, awards are meaningless in our profession. At one of those big awards ceremonies I was sitting beside Kenneth Horne, having a great old time. I really liked him. We both got awards that night and laughed ourselves silly, reminiscing. He gave a great speech, then stumbled off the podium, sat down beside me and dropped dead. That larger-than-life and lovely man was gone.

I went with him in the ambulance as the awards show continued. It was a terrible loss. I wish I had spent more time with him, and we had talked that evening about doing just that. I saw this as a wake-up call to enjoy every day.

Tin-pot trophies

The money I was making afforded us to buy our first house, which made me happy because in my head I was still, in small part, residing in parks and stations. Even though our flat was lavish in comparison, it felt temporary. Hampstead was where we chose to live. It has a real village feel about it, with its pubs and shops, but is still close to the city where we all worked. A lot of our chums lived there at the time too.

After I'd won the awards the phone stopped ringing. This fucked with my head. I tried to think of poor old Kenneth Horne's swift departure and use it as a way to calm myself down a bit.

It didn't work as the adrenalin was still roaring through me. I'd been through the mill in my early days of performing so I was trying desperately to drum up ideas. I was offered bits and pieces but nothing big enough to pay the bills. Eventually I decided to take the sketches and other stuff to a live audience, with a small group of chums, including Roland MacLeod, Chris Allen, Don Archell, Bill Hunter and Kenny Dyer, and a music combo to back up our craziness on stage. Colin McLennan and his company helped pull it together and I soon found myself too busy to think, a place I love to be. Rehearsals were hectic because time was tight – and we had a documentary crew following us. I was hellbent on trying to make the show different by including the audience in it, talking to them directly and involving them in as much spontaneous stuff as we could. We put in some sketches from my TV show, like the *Monster In A Box* and *The Travel Agent*. I knew that certain markets, Australia and Canada, would respond well to it because the telly show had been well received there and I was getting a ridiculous amount of interview requests from them.

Unfortunately we had to put the live show on hold: Barry and I had been asked to write a screenplay. But our stage time was nigh.

I spent any spare time reading or hanging out at jazz clubs. I've always found it easier to relax while I'm listening to jazz – ballet has this effect on me too.

A lot of my mates from the clubs couldn't drag their old ladies to a jazz gig. Johnny Speight loved Lauretta because she didn't talk through the music, and when she did talk she didn't bore the tits off him. We hung out regularly at Ronnie Scott's, a favourite club. Ronnie and I went way back to Jack Spot's. He really looked after us, and we brought all our chums to him. When he needed to go home we'd have them all back to our place for a jam and a jar. Spike was a constant at Ronnie's, too. Alan Clare was a proper piano player and Spike would be there whenever he was on the bill. Dudley, too, was a great pianist and would drop by to learn a thing or two from the big names who were playing.

London and Paris were two of the few places where big names in jazz would come to play. We saw Count Basie, Duke Ellington and all the giants, because now we had the funds to support our jazz habit. I never took that for granted – I would think back to the days when I was looking through windows to get a glimpse of Miles Davis playing because I hadn't any money to go in. A lot can be learned about dealing with success from hanging out with a veteran jazz player. They've seen it all, been through it all, and as long as they're working times are good. Harry 'Sweets' Edison, or Sweets as we knew him, became a mate and would stay with us when he visited London. Every time Lauretta or I poured him a brandy, he always said, 'I'm still in the game.'

The screenplay that Barry and I had been asked to write was *Every Home Should Have One*. My mate Ned Sherrin was producing it, based on an idea of Denis Norden's. Barry and I never thought of it as anything but a funny romp. Peter Sellers was offered the starring role but turned it down – he was too busy – and then it was offered to me. I was working on the live show but the offer was too good to pass up: the live show was as ready as it needed to be and a few more bob in the bank would help.

My agent, Kenneth, had reservations about me taking on the role, partly because I was so busy but also because he and I had discussed my holding off on doing any movies until the money and scripts were better than, or at least equal to, what I was already doing.

When I asked Peter Sellers what I should do, he said, 'Never turn down a movie unless a better one is on the table.' I felt that, between me and Barry, we could have something to work with.

Also, I didn't care whether this role was going to be successful or not, I just wanted to grow as a performer in front of a camera and make enough money to live the life my missus and I had become accustomed to! *Every Home Should Have One* was another vehicle for me to learn from and hone whatever skills I could use. I seem to remember spending more time talking about making the film than making it. You soon learn on a movie set

how small a cog in the big wheel you are. It is very much a director's medium. Rumours abounded from the set, linking me
romantically with the lovely Julie Ege, the female lead. None of
them was true but even Lauretta said she wouldn't blame me 'for
havin' a go'! We had a couple of nude scenes together and, to my
horror, my dick was very badly behaved. Julie laughed and said
she liked the respect it had for her. A great sense of humour for
a Swedish bird! Which I always called her, knowing she was from
Norway. That film was very well paid, and I scored some flash
clobber from it, gear from Mr Fish of Piccadilly himself. He
seemed to relish the fact that I'd wear whatever he threw at me.
The times called for a bit of splash.

The film came towards the end of my writing partnership
with Barry, not because we disliked each other or had nothing to
say, but I was getting more into performing and Barry was the
go-to guy for writing. We had both felt it coming and knew we'd
remain mates and work together again. When a writing partnership breaks up in our circles, people treat it like a divorce. For us
it was just what it was, although some of our pals would over-
think it and speak in hushed tones, all that nonsense. I had
custody of the scripts and Barry visited at weekends. Ever since
John, Graham and Tim had asked me to join them as an equal
in acting and cavorting on *1948*, things had been rolling fast but
it had never occurred to me that I wouldn't go back to writing
when the performing work ran out.

I keep writing regardless of acting gigs, and even as I write this
I'm thinking up ideas for a show. I hope you're still with me – you
are still there, darlings, aren't you? I'd get very lonely without you.

The *1948* boys were all ex-university and I was like a scholarship kid, but they never made me feel inferior. I wasn't a doctor,
like Graham, and couldn't teach because I lacked the qualifica-
tions, but because most people watching us were on the same

dodgy boat as I was, education-wise, they could identify with my characters, which worked to my advantage.

We respected each other because we all had one show under our belts and were learning as we went along. They had done *I'm Sorry, I'll Read That Again* while Barry and I were banging away on *Round the Horne* and other stuff. We all brought our different experiences to the table. I was not as skilled a performer as the others but my freakish looks made me stand out. I was idiosyncratically formed, wonderfully and fearfully shaped by life, and now I was using my appearance to get my foot in the door. People remembered seeing me in things. They often didn't recall the show but they hadn't forgotten my face, especially my eyEs. I was capitalising on my assets, like many a comedic performer before me. Harpo Marx was a decent-looking bloke: he found a wig and was up and running. Jack Benny used meanness as an ugly trait, with a violin as a crutch to great effect. I'm lucky to have it all built in.

THOUGHTS WHILE SHAVING GOD'S FACE

God made me in his own image
And I am sure he was trying to please
For in his own image he made me –
Even O. L. Jaggers agrees.

This morning I looked in my mirror
And I thought, as I looked upon God,
That if in his own image he made me
Then God looked remarkably odd.

David Frost had thought my 'wonky eyE' would scare off the punters but the exact opposite occurred. He seemed even more eager to drop me when we were all attending a test screening for the show for the suits to decide. The grey ones sat there and giggled. Frost looked tense, bless him!

Afterwards I was asked to step out and grab a cuppa while they had a chat. I was sure I would be out because, even though they laughed at my bits, I felt the suits would follow Frost's lead and panic. By the way, David is a good man and has always been good to me. I'm just a little worried for him! I wrote some stuff for *The Frost Report*. Johnny Speight wrote the bulk of it, and I'm proud that we brought Frankie Howerd into the show because he was considered at the time to be washed up. He was older than us lot, but made me laugh really hard.

ODE TO PONTIUS

Hooray for Sir Pontius Kaak, my friends
Who invented the bicycle pump,
A small step for mankind perhaps,
But a huge intellectual jump.
Considering that when his pump he patented,
The bicycle had not been invented.

David Frost was in a position to make or break me as a performer at this time, and as much as I admire him and never look back in anger, I do look sideways in suspicion! I had been through the mill before. The suits decided not only that I should stay but that more sketches should be constructed for me. I couldn't believe it and still don't – 'tis but a fickle wind that blows in our chosen field.

I never take any audience for granted, thinking they will laugh as soon as I walk on stage. When they do laugh I'm amazed and feel like a confidence trickster who has done a three-card trick and always blows town fast before his victim catches on.

The documentary *One Pair of EyEs* aired around this time, just when everything was getting hectic. It was originally intended to be all about me but I suggested it would be more interesting if we were to film me chatting with people I had either worked with and/or admired. Shooting began with me walking through Margate's Dreamland, where it had all started for me as a performer, then moving to different locations showing where I had come from. To my complete horror, when it aired, instead of being light and fun, it was dark and full of me interrupting people I loved – Peter Sellers, Dudley Moore, Eric Morecambe, Johnny Speight, Barry Took and Annie Ross. I was so embarrassed that I'd ever got any of them involved and only hoped they didn't see it. Another valuable lesson learned on the treacherous path of showbiz. Luckily the *Marty* shows were getting good notices, which balanced things a bit.

Also around this time Pye Records were planning to put out an album of songs and sketches from *Marty*, with the great music of Ken Jones who had written our signature tune. At the same time I was asked to do another record for Decca that would include a collection of songs written by Denis King and John Junkin, who had written all the funny songs for the show. I was now a recording artist! My favourite song we did was called 'La Sauce': I was singing, with a daft French accent, lyrics consisting of the ingredients listed on the back of an HP sauce bottle.

I took the Decca recording very seriously because I knew I could duck the critics by saying it was a comedy record and supposed to be funny, the old empty trumpet-case routine. But the songs we put in were great and worth the hard work. Just to be placed in a record bin close to Aretha Franklin made it all worth while. My dad had died before I became known as a performer but I think he would have liked my silly songs: he liked to sing silly words to well-known songs, and drive people nuts when they tried to sing along. The song 'The Very Thought Of You' became

The very thought of glue and I forget to poo
The very ordinary things a dad ought to do . . .

Although my dad died suddenly quite young, at sixty-four in 1969, he achieved so much in his life, creating everything from nothing. I still think of him as my biggest fan: the song on the radio or my telly show airing after he died didn't matter because I feel he is always with me, nudging me with a wry wink. I have always thought I, too, would die young: I can never see myself as an old man, not because I don't want to but because I just don't feel my distance will be that far.

One of the highlights of my time with my dad was at the World Cup at Wembley in 1966. He scored some great seats from some bloke he knew and Tim-Brooke Taylor, he and I all went and had the time of our lives, a hundred thousand fans screaming for a couple of hours. It was a particularly special treat for my dad: not only did we beat the best team in the world, they happened to be Germans. My dad and his generation never forgot or came close to forgiving the Germans for their atrocities towards Jews. It was the most exciting match I have ever seen, loads of goals, extra time and a hat-trick by Geoff Hurst, the hero of a nation.

I had always wanted to be black, beautiful, talented and surrounded by stunning birds, like Miles Davis, but I remember seeing my dad sitting in a pub after we went to that match and thinking, If I become a bit like him, that wouldn't be bad either.

FOREVER

Going through life snapping at each new NOW,
Making good memories when we get old,
Wanting to make sure it is well stocked for looking back,
There today, here tomorrow each new father his son told

Living is an ephemeral art,
To die should be our sole adventure,
For life is as brief as a buck fly's fart
But death is something we have for ever.

Doing my own show was satisfying in every way, but especially in terms of creativity. I can't say often enough how lucky I was to have the talent surrounding me but also the freedom to do whatever we wanted. That was never to happen again.

When you are a writer you sweat as you watch other people working from your script. When you're a performer, you have someone to blame. When it works, there's no satisfaction quite like it. Not that what I'm doing is new or any different from what went before. There will always be so much of other people's influences in our work that without them we couldn't exist. Eventually they become part of us.

Comedy is intuitive, and the more you rationalise it, the less you can do it. I always seem to be on the verge of panic: that is the impetus that keeps me doing what I do. If I felt secure I would simply repeat what I have done that works. It's exhilarating not knowing if something will get a laugh. I like to go with my instincts, and if it feels funny, it mostly is. That's why I'm a comedy writer rather than a plumber or a bank clerk. Life is either absurd or tragic. I laugh at it – my way to keep fear at bay. I do not believe in pathos: a comic only attracts a warm response from his audience if he is basically a warm person.

My first series of shows came and went in a flash, and before I knew it I was starting the second, with a special called *Marty Amok* at the end.

I started to see the pattern in my immediate future, workwise: my mission was to make it different but always funny. No easy task. Writing, group writing especially, can be very difficult to pull off: the result seems funny when you read it but falls flat when you see it on the screen.

There are tougher jobs, I know.

MARTY FELDMAN.
(BBC 1, 9.20)

"MARTY" 1st Series

NO. 1

Ticket Agency.
Beethoven Quickie.
The Bishop.
Organisation Organisation.
Police 6⅞.
At the Vet.
Night Life.

NO. 2

Travel Agency.
Tonight in Westminster.
Lady Chaterley Quickie.
The Greek God Zeus.
Table Top Battle.   3'30"
Script Conference.
Nursery Sketch.
Wiffenpoof Song.

NO. 3

The Weatherman	0'31"
The Headmaster	2'15"
Football Int	3'09"
Salome Quickie	0'38"
Traffic Problems	1'23"
The Epilogue	2'47"
Funny He Never Married	4'15"
The Yech	5'24"
Mavis Wavertree	0'40"

NO. 4

Hieroglyphics	1'55"
Dr. Jekyll	0'50"
Football Q	0'32"
P.C. Ogmore	5'11"
Speak Your Weight	2'24"
The Wedding	2'52"
YO.BO.Ballet	3'46"
My Fathers Shirt	1'50"
Marriage Guidance.	

NO. 5

Art Gallery	0'43"
Eyeferroi	3'06"
The Gnome.	4'40"
Playground Quickie	1'59"
Sentry	2'47"
Black & White Minstrels	5'08"
Like Father	4'56"
Opera Without Music	3'39"
Doonican Q	0'58"
Lord of the Flies	4'38"

NO. 6

Dixie Opening	0'32"
Hospital	4'00"
Driving Instructor	1'15"
Country Pub	2'20"
Back Chat	3'05"
Ronald J God	2'59"
Woodworm	3'47"
At the Florist	7'25"

On 9 November 1970, I almost ended my career in front of the Queen Mum. I was invited to perform at *The Royal Variety Performance*. I despise everything about the monarchy and feel embarrassed about the turmoil it has created in the world. However, the show was a benefit concert for a cause I believed in and it was a dream come true to appear at the Palladium where I had seen Danny Kaye. It seemed like only yesterday that I was flogging jokes by the stage door to anyone who would have them.

During my sketch I divested myself of my clothing, upsetting my mum and Phil the Greek (Prince Philip). I was told that nobody takes their clothes off in front of royalty, though Phil must have done. Where else could Anne and Charles have come from? Maybe there's been another Immaculate Conception that we don't know about. The audience were afraid to laugh but I had a right old time. Dionne Warwick, who was also on the bill, was introduced as 'a person of colour with a distinctive voice'! Oh, England, my England, no more. I was stalked by a female member of the Black Theatre Company of Prague. She had been told that I was a star and offered free fellatio and other such treats, which I declined. Even though the idea of getting a blow job separated from Mum by a curtain was tempting.

THE LONDON PALLADIUM

Monday, November 9th, 1970

Bernard Delfont, Leslie A. MacDonnell C.B.E., & Reg Swinson M.B.E.

tender their congratulations to

Mr. Marty Feldman

on being invited to appear before

HER MAJESTY THE QUEEN MOTHER

on the occasion of the

ROYAL VARIETY PERFORMANCE

in aid of

The Variety Artistes' Benevolent Fund

WANKER PRODUCTIONS

1600 North Highland Avenue ● Hollywood, California 90028

(213) 467-2019

Mr. James Gilbert
BBC TV CENTER
Wood Lane
London W.12
ENGLAND

Dear Sir or Madman:

I understand that you recently showed the half-hour
compilation, 'Marty in Montreux'.

Is it possible to obtain a print or tape of this show, purely
for my own records? You see, the work that you do is the
Only evidence you have that you ever existed.

I have almost nothing to prove that I exist. Obviously,
I would be willing to pay whatever costs that would be
incurred by striking a print or a tape. Please help me prove
my existence, Jim, provided that you still exist -- God knows
Dennis Main-Wilson exists. He probably knows where all the
bodies are buried, since he probably buried them.

My love to anyone who will accept it and we'll meet again
from the song of the same name recorded by Vera Lynn and
available on Decca.

Yours relatively sincerely,

Marty Feldman

"MARTY" 2nd Series

NO. 1

Toulouse Lautrec	0'20"
3-Minute Coach Trip	3'39"
Tech Hitch Q	0'10"
Football Commentator	4'15"
The Chase	1'19"
The Golfer	6'30"
Newspaper Ex	1'15"
Ped Busters	11'55"
Closing Titles	0'50"

NO. 2

Dixon Opening	00'55"
The Post Office	4'25"
Film Parade	7'07"
Peking Q	0'29"
Serbian Restaurant	4'50"
The Stuntman	4'58"
Richard III	0'19"
Seance	6'48"
Dixon Close	0'35"
Closing Titles	0'50"

NO. 3

Coughing Q	2'00"
TV Decency	4'10"
Old Boy Net	0'30"
Frost Obituary	3'40"
The Phone Call	1'10"
Ballet Dancer	4'55"
The Danny Gruntfuttoch	8'53"
Christmas Song	4'22"
Closing Titles	0'50"

NO. 4

Z Cars Opening.	
Insurance Sketch.	
Nelson Q.	
Supermidwife.	3'00"
Flicka Q.	
Home Movies.	3'00"
The World Tomorrow.	
Henry V.	
My Yiddesne Momma.	
The New Servant.	
Closing Titles.	
Flying Rabbi.	

NO. 5

Mutiny on the Bounty.	
Unwelcome Guests.	
Clothists.	
I'm Taking Your Name.	
Welsh Mining Disaster.	
Camel Song.	
H.P. Sauce.	
Britain for Sale.	
Regular Clergy.	4'00"
Enoch Powell.	
Second Opinion.	
Closing Titles.	

NO. 6

Call Marty Feldman	0'20"
Wine Press.	
Fly Quickie.	
Shell Q.	
Sunday Driver	5'00"
D.N.A.	
Shell Q.	
Change.	
Shell Q.	
Punch and Judy.	
Closing Sequence Marty intro backstage.	
Closing Titles.	

1969 was a massive blur because so much was going on between all the work, my dad dying, moving to a new house and feeling like a nomad. I certainly wasn't slowing down, as per the doctor's advice. As well as planning and rehearsing stuff for the live show and tour in Australia, I accepted acting roles in two BBC plays for *Comedy Playhouse* called *Double Bill*. They were serious shows and serious work, it was my first foray into drama. Lauretta was very busy too because she had to organise it for me. I know how *I* did it, but how she does it I will never know. She's the Beauty behind the Beast. I was also doing a lot of press interviews and photo shoots, which take a lot of time. The interviews are hard to do because the published articles are often full of shit and someone's bound to get hurt. You can't imagine how many stories I've told about my eyEs. I get so bored with the questions I start making shit up.

I was feeling the urge to do something different involving live shows. I wanted to pull as many of my pals together as I could and take a revue to towns where people were tired of watered-down music-hall acts.

Meanwhile Lauretta and I went to Antibes on a holiday and asked Eric Idle and his new bride, Lyn, to join us, with our other pals Anne and Ted Levy. We would show Eric and Lyn a good time as we four had all been there before, and then they would be off honeymooning. We were all chums and it didn't seem strange to us to be travelling together, but with Eric's and my profiles being fairly high, much was made of it in the rags. They wanted to believe we had all gone mad, like they did when the Beatles went away together, except we weren't the Beatles – although Eric was getting close! Eric is one of those people you meet and love right away. His talent is immense: he is a great actor and comedian and a really talented musician too.

I thought he and I would make a good duo in a live setting and when we returned home I became consumed with trying to put together something that would work and be fun. I still wanted to do the live show we had prepared for Australia but a different idea was bubbling away. It centred around a circus-type road show that would travel by train or in a caravan of trucks, making a spectacle of our arrival at each location. We would pitch a big tent for a week just outside towns and put on a modern variety show. I even came up with a show title, *Atlantic Crossing*: we would start in America and Canada, then travel around Europe, beginning with a week in Ireland. The shows would embrace our common interests as the cast would be made up of players from each side of the Atlantic. It would have two well-known American comedic stars, such as Bill Cosby and Carol Burnett, plus me and another British comedian, ideally Eric Idle or Dudley Moore, both of whom had great musical talent. We'd also have a crack band of American and English musicians. I was even planning to apprentice myself to a circus and learn how to be a proper clown, maybe even how to protect my body from all the abuse I'd subjected it to. I wanted to work with talented, adventurous people in front of a live audience, with huge chunks of audience participation. I have it all written out and hope still to do it.

As soon as I was getting to like the idea of becoming more of a live act and hoping to erase the horrible memories of past live performances, the phone rang and my agent told me that Lew Grade was offering a show with some very attractive elements. It would primarily be aimed at breaking me on American telly.

Larry Gelbart – whom I'd met and thought was a smart bloke – was to produce it and I was free to choose whomever I wanted to work with. First choice without a doubt was Spike.

The money was fantastic and I immediately jumped at it even though I felt my telly sketch ideas were running a bit thin. Bringing in new writers, though, like Barry Levinson, and using graphics by Terry Gilliam, whom I'd seen in New York doing some underground show a few years before, made me feel we could pull it off. I was also free to have whichever musical acts I liked.

My head was soon on fire with ideas. The only downside? It was to be an hour-long show. I had never done that before and couldn't imagine sustaining anybody's interest for that long. I put up a fight and lost, then saw it as a chance to bring some of my favourite performers together, as I'd wanted to do with the live show. I figured this show could help set up markets for the revue in America and beyond. *The Marty Feldman Comedy Machine*, as the show was to be called, even had a revue feel about it. I also saw it as a stepping stone on the way to roping Eric into the live show.

The talent I was after were all getting busy with their own shows. The Pythons were up and running and Tim Brooke-Taylor about to launch his very successful show *The Goodies*.

Spike was always busy but, much to my delight, became available and I took full advantage of his talents. Peter Cook and I had some great ideas but he, too, was busy. Everyone was doing their own stuff to great success.

We really worked our arses off on that show. I broke my wrist and arm doing my own stunts but we had a lot of fun. You never know when you're doing a show like that how people will respond to it: times change so fast. I'd included several silent elements, hoping it would do well in any country.

There were great bits in it but, alas, they were too few and overall it was not as good as it might have been. I had been right that it was too long. However, Lew Grade was sure it was going to be big and even sent a reel to Montreux for award consideration.

It won the big prize, the Golden Rose, but I was too exhausted to care.

I took a money gig in Italy around this time, which pissed off everyone around me, but I didn't want to be in the country when that show was being aired. I even lied and said I had to stay longer to avoid picking up the award in Switzerland. Lauretta thought it best that I stayed away in case I said something nasty.

I was drinking too much and generally feeling low but, as always, Lauretta steered the ship through the storms. I was having terrible dreams about death and I felt lousy. I was too old to die young and too young to grow up. Or in fact to know any differently.

I kept working: I appeared on telly shows that were shown in America, and ended up being asked to do *Golddiggers*, the summer replacement for *The Dean Martin Show*, which Dean was presenting anyway. It was made in Britain by NBC to show in the US, and was a smart show to be on: it clicked with people. I didn't know that Dean was nuts. Working with him was as strange an experience as I've had on a show. We met for the first time in front of the camera when it was clear that this would be a one-take affair: that any further takes would be captured while he was on the golf course. I had heard this was how he did it but it is only when you're doing it that you realise how crazy it all is.

I was unaware that I was described as a hit in America until calls were coming in for interviews. I really didn't know what to think. We'd had no plans to move to America although France was starting to sound good, but the idea of running away from it all, having worked my way to where I was, wasn't hip. It's easier to hang out with friends in pubs than to take on new work – although with the *Comedy Machine* I'd been lucky enough to do both. In America *Comedy Machine* was getting good notices and offers started to come in. Combined with *Golddiggers*, I began to think it was time to go west and see what I could get going there.

Offers always come my way and I should learn to breathe like Lauretta tells me and enjoy the moments. I was asked to do all sorts of things because people thought I was 'in', as my agent would say. I agreed to choreograph a ballet for the Hamburg Opera House. My agent and others were shocked but it was so different it appealed to me. I've always loved ballet so that seemed like a great way to pass my time. Besides, there were always dance pieces in my shows, like the Irving Davies Dancers doing a ballet-style warm-up for Spike's nonsense song.

I was lured back to work for the BBC with a show to be called *Marty Back Together Again*. I felt the need to cleanse the collective palate of the bad taste my last show had left in my mouth. Mostly it was a way of working with my pal Johnny Speight and to see if we could offer something different but really funny. We thought we could. Initially we were offered a long series but opted to do four half-hour programmes.

I liked a silent short we did called *Marty Abroad*, which had aired around the time that *Every Home* was released. I got to do as much silent stuff as anyone could take.

Johnny and I were determined to go out with a bang. Only he and I knew that this would be my last sketch show on British telly. I would do another show, if offered, but not in the sketch format, which was unique and of its time and I felt the time was almost up. We did some adventurous stuff, the cast was different and the material felt new, even fresh. I was finally getting back to what I was good at: short sketches that didn't rely heavily on dialogue.

The show that Johnny and I hatched in the pub became the show that was aired: we wanted warts and all. Working at Ealing Studios was inspiring, and I consider Johnny's writing to be on a par with Dickens – I really rate Dickens. Even in a comedy setting, Johnny's work had a direct and emotional tone. Derek

Griffiths, a fantastic singer, mover and actor, was a great cast member and I really clicked with him. Johnny and I had known each other for years. He was a drummer back in the days when we were hustling to break into the music scene. We shared a lot of interests but our love of jazz was our bond. We also had a small person called George Claydon who, at his tallest, measured twenty-one inches, and James Villiers, who measured six foot four.

It is impossible to know or learn what makes people laugh.

Duke Ellington was once asked what jazz meant and he said, 'If you have to ask you will never know.'

We felt that if we could make each other, the rest of the cast and the crew laugh, we'd have done enough. I love words as a writer but when it comes to my acting I prefer to use fewer. I am a visual comic and the cast we assembled were the same. I got a bit nervous that we might either repeat older ideas or be copying what was current. Time to put these shows together was hard to come by and trying to write, rehearse and perform simultaneously was difficult.

I knew what I wanted for the show: I was not primarily concerned with prodding the audience's social conscience or gaining the critics' approval. I just wanted to make people laugh.

I was concerned, too, that Johnny might not have enough material for a series of shows. I shouldn't have worried but my track record led me to believe that I needed to take more control and be more accountable for the end results. I used the music of Tom Lehrer to link the sketches. John Junkin and Denis King were great songwriters for my limited talents but I was intent on not repeating myself.

Somehow it all came together, as these things rarely do.

Dennis Main Wilson was our producer and left us to do what we did. He once hired a huge bloody crane that sat unused on one of the sets we were working on. When I saw him, I asked him what it was for. He said, 'You never know, Mart, it's a funny old business, comedy.' We never used it.

We spent as much time in the pub as we did making the show: the weather was dreadful and we waited around a lot for the skies to clear. We knew it was triumph of content over form and we were all ready to be exploited. We had a sketch called *Dwarfo* that George loved. In it big Jim would lead wee George around on a leash. They played two ordinary blokes doing mundane things, going to the races, the pub, wherever. Nobody made any remarks and carried out their business while these two characters walked among them. We all laughed when we were writing it, but when we saw it, none of us did, and it was scrapped. We had a strong producer in Dennis so we were not pressured to air everything we shot, which was a relief.

A highlight of that short series was working with Tom Lehrer, whom I admired greatly. We chose a bunch of his satirical songs and Derek, a great musician, was the perfect partner for me to do them with. Tom even came on board to help us. 'Pollution' and 'The Vatican Rag' came off well. Years later Tom told me the show had opened doors for him in Britain. I was thrilled.

With *Marty*, *Marty Amok*, *Marty Abroad* and now *Marty Back Together Again*, it felt very much like it was time for Marty to be unseen and unheard so we decided to book the tour of Australia we had longed to do.

Our home life at this time couldn't have been better, but it would be a long trip: we kept putting it off. Eventually we had one bloody great big party at our house, not realising it would be the very last party we would ever have there. All of our chums gathered and we had a fantastic time. A nice send-off from a truly great bunch of people.

One of my fondest memories from this time was the result of a series of events that involved Lauretta, Peter Cook, Dudley Moore, Francis Bacon and myself. We all lived relatively near each other and one night on my way home from writing with Barry I passed a gallery that was having a do. I could hear a jazz band inside, playing a great version of 'A Night in Tunisia' so I wandered in and found myself among an interesting-looking bunch of people.

I was offered a cocktail and accepted. I had a bit of a poke around and didn't like much of the artist's work but there was a bit of a buzz about the place. After a few more complimentary cocktails I decided to head home. Just as I was leaving, I was stopped by a drunk man with a strange accent and an odd yet friendly demeanour. He asked if I would be interested in sitting for him as he would love to paint a portrait of me. I was quite sure he was hitting on me and I coolly declined, saying my wife was waiting for me. He was very polite and asked if he could give me his number. I said yes and we parted.

The next morning I told Lauretta about it and she said I should throw the number away – the man had been trying to pick me up. I told her he'd written Francis as his name. What if he was Bacon, one of her favourite painters?

She told me to catch on: Bacon did not paint people.

Many months later while I was working with Peter Cook on some writing ideas, we joined Dudley in the pub and made a day of it. We poured out of the place hammered and tried to remember who we were and where we lived. Somehow we got lost and ended up at another art gallery – they seemed to be everywhere back then.

We were all offered cocktails by a person who foolishly thought we needed them. I spotted my old pal Francis standing at a distance and pointed him out to Peter, who knew my story because I had become obsessed with the what-ifs. Bacon's work was fetching high prices and it would have been fun if he'd painted a portrait of me and I hadn't told Lauretta, just invited her to a gallery and pretended it was no big deal. Lauretta loved him because he was Irish, openly gay and proud, and his paintings tended to have an anti-religious theme. Why wouldn't she love him? Anyway old drunky McCookie told more drunky McMoore that Francis wanted to paint me but I'd thrown away his number. Without hesitation, Dudley went straight up to Bacon and told him that Marty was now ready to be painted. Bacon told Dudley that he had never seen or talked to me in his life and that his chums must be winding him up. We were all unknowns then, their film *Bedazzled* had just been shot and they didn't have high hopes for it and I had just started work on *At Last the 1948 Show*. So nobody, especially Bacon, thought we were anything but a bunch of drunken wankers. Which in hindsight was sadly true. Dudley got really mad at Pete and me and stormed off and we didn't see him for weeks.

A couple of days later I found a note in my mailbox from Francis Bacon asking me to please call him or drop in at his home studio. I was convinced Lauretta, Pete or Dud was winding me up, but I threw caution to the wind and, on my way home from writing with Barry, I called at his home studio. I knocked on the door and was let in by a rather strange bloke who left me to wait for ages in the hallway.

Bacon finally appeared and was very apologetic. He explained that he was readying a show and his agent had been hounding him. I told him I didn't want to disturb him, and before I knew it I was sitting sipping cognac surrounded by his work. He was such a lovely man and he told me that after the night when Dud had approached him at the party he did remember me but was too embarrassed to do anything about it. It turned out that one of his pals was a fan of *Round the Horne*, and when he told Bacon I was one of the writers of *Julian and Sandy*, he was very excited to meet me.

He sat there sipping his drink and would suddenly burst into dialogue from our show. Hours passed and when I got up to use the bathroom I realised I was plastered. We were singing and making plans to do a show together, he playing himself and me playing the old Francis Bacon, and we would be *Francis Not Francis* the crime stoppers! We had a great time. As I was leaving, he couldn't stop hugging me and I was saying all sorts of silly things when he suddenly stopped and said, 'Mart, we've spent all this time together and I still haven't painted you. You must take a painting with you.' I declined his kind gesture but he just grabbed one, thrust it at me and threw me out the door with it. It was quite big and I had to get home, almost too drunk to carry it, but I made it.

I woke up the next morning with Lauretta leaning over me, insisting I tell her where I got the painting. I told her Francis gave it to me because he'd felt bad about not recognising me and then forgetting to paint me while we were hanging out yesterday.

She called me a fucking liar and threatened to destroy it unless I told her the truth.

A few weeks before this, Lauretta had taken a call from my agent saying Fellini wanted to meet with me about a project. When I'd got home and she told me, I wouldn't believe her even though she insisted that she wasn't winding me up. I never called my agent – and found out later that it was true. Now she thought I was winding *her* up. I came downstairs and she was still threatening to throw the painting out.

I tried again to tell her what a great bloke he was but she was having none of it. So I told her I'd take it back to him and she dared me to do just that. Later that day I headed over to Peter Cook's house with the painting to try out some writing ideas. After we'd worked for a while we decided to call it a day and I asked him if he would hang on to the painting until I figured out what to do with it. He agreed, and we headed off to the pub for a quickie before tea. We got very well oiled and Cookie decided that the best thing to do with the painting was to bring it back to Bacon and hope he'd be OK with it.

We made our way back to Francis's house with the painting in the pouring rain – I threw my coat over it and we took turns to carry it, trying not to drop it. When we finally got to his house and rang his doorbell, we found that nobody was at home. Pete thought the best idea was to leave the painting at the door with a note saying, 'Thanks but I simply couldn't accept it.'

I said we should leave it at his back door because it had an awning and we didn't have a pen or paper and it was fucking lashing on us.

Pete helped me over the wall, then threw the painting over to me and I placed it carefully under the awning, leaning against the back door with my coat still on it. The painting was a distorted portrait of maybe a man, maybe even Bacon himself, and I figured a spot of water couldn't make it any more distorted. I tried to climb back over the wall but couldn't manage it. Lanky

Pete had to scramble over and push me back. I was sure I'd broken some part of my body.

When Pete was on my side of the wall again, he straightened himself up and said, 'All right, Mart, see you tomorrow, mate,' and was gone.

I never heard from Francis, and Pete never spoke of it again, but every time Sotheby's puts another of his paintings up for sale, Lauretta always says, 'What if, Mart!'

SKIN DEEP

Some people wear their skin outside
Though it creases when they grin,
But I wear my skin inside
Because it makes my legs look thin.
Besides, outside my inside skin
I can stand and just peer in
And I've got the slightest doubt
If I wear my skin inside
I can stop it ever wearing out.

We had first come to California in 1962 when I was dragging Lauretta from state to state, following Groucho Marx on his concert tour and always seeming to miss him. We would land in some town, find ourselves consumed and titillated by our surroundings and lose all sense of time. We loved California and Los Angeles in particular. We had a couple of mates there and were happy to catch up and be shown the bright lights and sights. There was a sense of great wealth and even greater poverty existing side by side. Also, the light can only be experienced in person.

I have often said if you want to make a living cutting pineapples go to Hawaii, and if you want to make a living in showbiz, there is but one town that has all the factories and that is Los Angeles.

ART!

To argue that starvation will produce great art
Is akin to suggesting if you eat broken glass
You will shit diamonds.
On the other hand, note to the rich:
If you eat diamonds you will certainly shit broken glass.

In 1962, when we docked in the port of New York and took our leave of the *Queen Mary*, we soon realised we'd landed in the middle of a massive protest march: the Cuban Missile Crisis was in full-on mode. I loved it and was shouting my support and piercing the sky with my clenched fist, like Che Guevara, when Lauretta realised, from observing others, that I should be against it and shouldn't look so happy.

It was a very scary time to land in America. We watched it on the news from our telly in a tiny hotel room and wondered what would happen. New York seemed like an obvious target and as things cranked up we decided the only thing to do was enjoy a show or two and stay drunk for as long as we could.

The irony for us was that we had come to America rather hastily because I had abruptly quit a decent paying gig with Barry on *Bootsie and Snudge*. I was starting to lose my marbles a bit, freaked out and told Barry I was sorry but I needed a break. I booked two tickets on the *Queen Mary* before I told Lauretta because I was sure she would talk me out of it. Nobody was best pleased but Lauretta thought it was the only thing to do and the next day we were on our way, with limited funds and no idea if I'd have a gig when we returned.

We spent our first five nights seeing John Coltrane and his incredible band play two sets per night at Birdland. It took Lauretta that many shows to finally get it and enjoy it!

We also spent time checking out all the famous spots, like the Village Vanguard and the Village Gate, and the venues on 52nd Street. The feeling around these great places was similar to London's vibe in the late sixties: things were changing and moving on.

Rock 'n' roll was building steam, as was folk music, which was booming because of the civil-rights movement and the Cuban situation. There was plenty to shout about. Greenwich Village was the hub of the folk movement and we had a chum who knew where to go. It was Café This and That, and had a very French/F. Scott feel. Hot little birds running around with flyers and little clothing, and chaps with turtle-neck sweaters and odd facial-hair developments.

We were taken to one place where a big man called Dave Van Ronk sang and blew us away. One night we saw Sonny Terry and Brownie McGhee and the next was Odetta. We were invited to a party some place where we got to see Pete Seeger – everyone was talking about him and he certainly lived up to his chat. He introduced a wiry little chap who sang a song called 'Hard Times in New York Town' and I thought I was going to pass out from the greatness of it all. We saw Edith Piaf at Carnegie Hall and Count Basie with his roaring band but that one song really did my nut in.

We felt like we were the last people in the world to hear all this great music – everyone around us was rather blasé about it. Folk artists were supposed to sing songs about old-timey things, like the changing of the leaves and the elves found beneath them, but these people were all writing great poetry about current situations and we were well impressed.

We saw the wiry little guy again the next night at a tiny club, which was no bigger than an average kitchen. He walked on, did a few songs and fucked off without saying a word. The next person said, 'Bobby Dylan, everyone,' like it happened all the time. Just like Miles Davis, he let the work speak for itself. It helped take our minds off all the impending gloom.

We met some great people and everything seemed to be cheap or free. I bought a cheapo typewriter because I was inspired. Lauretta, ever my rock, secluded me and off I went again with my fingers!

STONE TO GRASS

The square I build upon the oblong
Will not stand firm upon this distracted earth.
Having promised myself a prayer, what should I ask?
Only grant that each and all my maudlin hurts
Are not proportionate to my just deserts.
Myself the Gingerbread idiot
Heedless of dusty clock beats
Built my squares upon the oblongs,
Believed the improbable machine to be equal.
Before Archangels said to me my personal word
And guaranteed my fate,
I minded the aggregate bone and thought it would stand firm
Upon this distracted earth, now living badly
But wanting to be remembered well.
I ask that all my hurts are not proportionate to my just deserts.

When we returned to America after the last house party in Hampstead, things were very different: no missile crisis, no great jazz or folk music. In Los Angeles, the songs being played on the radio were about getting it on, keeping it on and staying together. The sun was a welcome background.

On the flight over, Lauretta had an overwhelming feeling that we would never return to London or England again. I thought that was a bit strong but her hunches were usually spot on. We did go back to do some telly and press, but she'd meant we'd never go back and live there. We were greeted at Los Angeles airport by a young bloke from the William Morris Agency called Michael Ovitz, who was to take us to our digs and look after us.

I will always remember sitting in the back of the car with the sun splitting the early-morning sky and this bloke going on about how my telly shows had changed his life. I wanted him to stop but we soon learned there was as good a chance of that happening as putting a scarf over the sun to block its rays.

Lauretta and I were optimistic. We had felt that January 1970 in London had had a strange ending feel about it.

The Beatles were done, and most of the comedy troupes and writers had dispersed. It had felt like we were being urged gently out of the nest into the big world.

Los Angeles felt like the big world. It was like bursting into a Technicolor screening of a film having just spent a few hours watching grainy black-and-white 1940s footage. Back in England at one of those horrible awards shows, I'd met Sheldon Leonard, the actor, director and producer, who'd said some really nice things about *Marty* and that he'd written to the head of NBC and told them they should snap me up. I was honoured and believed him. I was even more thrilled to find out when we got to LA that he was a man of his word. Meetings were set up and we didn't have much time to take in the town. I was only going to be in LA for a couple of weeks before taking off to do the live *Marty Amok* show in Australia. At long last!

I did turns on telly, mostly rehashing old bits on shows like *Flip Wilson* and *Merv Griffin*. I made a bunch of dough from showing up and not saying much on *Hollywood Squares*, which I was happy to do any time.

I met all sorts of people, who mostly said kind things and compared my work to my hero Buster Keaton's, which made me uncomfortable. I knew why they said it. I wore my love for him on my sleeve and in my shows. They had seen a sketch I did called *The Wheel*, where I was chasing a spare wheel from my car all over the place. It was silent and speeded up, and I wore a very Keatonesque hat.

Keaton had genius and I had talent: comparing us was like comparing Bach to an ordinary organist. But I took it as a compliment. Keaton had died only four years before, so he was still fresh on many older people's minds.

In Los Angeles I was lucky enough to make good business contacts. An agent asked me who I'd like to work with. I sputtered, 'Gene Wilder,' and was about to add a few more names when the agent told me he represented him and that we should call him then and there. Suddenly I was on the phone with this very polite, soft-spoken man who told me that he had been lying in bed very late one night and was flicking through the telly channels when he'd stumbled upon *The Marty Feldman Comedy Machine*. He watched a couple of minutes of the show, then sprang out of bed and scribbled on a yellow notepad 'Young Frankenstein'.

He said he didn't know why he'd written it but thought I had to be in the mix somewhere. We spoke for ages about our shared love of *The Bride of Frankenstein* and about how it could have been so much better. I had met my match in my passion for films. At some point in our conversation I looked out of the agent's window and saw a huge docile-looking man. I said to Gene, 'I think I may have found your Monster.' That man was Peter Boyle, an actor also represented by that agent. I decided that Mike Medavoy would be my agent too.

Gene told me he was writing something and really wanted me to be in it. I had been offered a series but really felt that he was going to come through with something. He knew I was going to tour in Australia and asked where to send me stuff he was working on. When we finally got there, a script was waiting for me.

Gene wrote that when he'd got off the phone after our call, he couldn't stop writing and soon came up with my character

Igor – or eyE-Gor, for comic effect. I was to be the assistant to Gene's Dr Frederick Frankenstein. Gene had asked Mel Brooks to direct and co-write the screenplay and he had accepted. It was a dream come true.

Lauretta and I had seen Gene in *Bonnie and Clyde* and I'd told her that I thought Gene would be a star. We continued to be impressed with him in Mel's wonderful film *The Producers* and in *Willy Wonka & the Chocolate Factory*. He is truly fantastic.

I had heard he was working with Mel on *Blazing Saddles* and was looking forward to seeing that too. He had been on my mind for a while but so too had Mel Brooks. I'd never imagined I would work with him either.

It felt quite surreal to be sitting at the other end of the world reading Gene's first draft of his script and realising that not only was Gene going to be in it, but Mel would be directing and the gentle-looking giant Peter Boyle would be along for the ride.

The live shows went really well in Australia and the people were lovely.

We did a show for telly too, which included footage of me at the Sydney Zoo talking to the animals and fooling around. We planned to go back one day and see the whole country, get a bit of a far-off culture into us.

We soon came down to earth when on our second to last show we found out that we owed a lot of money in tax that we were sure we had paid back in England. The earnings from the tour plus the advance on *Young Frankenstein* eventually paid off our debt but left us skint on our return to Tinseltown. Still, the future was looking bright.

Back in LA, we moved into a nice house in the hills near the Hollywood sign and I was starting to get ready for my role in *Young Frankenstein*. We had been spending every day in hotels since leaving London and we were happy to be in a house, even if it wasn't our own. Lauretta soon made it home. Although I was at work right away, there were plenty of days off before shooting began and we had a few gatherings with the people we knew.

I found a regular local football club and joined it, then played on a team with some mates, a bunch of waiters and other actors. We had a blast. In Hollywood an average football team could include anyone, and Rod Stewart and George Best were just two who showed up for a kick-around. In England when a couple of famous people got together everything would go crazy with photographers showing up, but not in LA. We played some great charity football matches in the States and in England. At one match in England I played with the Pythons against a crowd of other nuts.

Combining national past-times!

ALL-STAR FOOTBALL

all proceeds to

SUNSHINE HOMES FOR CHILDREN

(Variety Club of Great Britain)

AND EAST HAM UTD. FC

MARTY FELDMAN XI

v.

MONTY PYTHON XI

To be played at

EAST HAM UTD. FC GROUND
MANOR WAY, EAST HAM, E.6

on

SUNDAY, 21st OCTOBER, 1973

K.O. 3 p.m.

Entrance by programme 25p

THE TEAMS WILL BE SELECTED FROM THE FOLLOWING

MARTY FELDMAN	TV, Films	ALAN INGRAM	East Ham FC
IAN McSHANE	Films	HARRY CRIPPS	Millwall FC
TERRY JONES	"Monty Python"	DENNIS BURNETT	Millwall FC
MICHAEL PALIN	"Monty Python"	NORMAN MEDHURST	Chelsea FC
ERIC IDLE	"Monty Python"	PETER LORENZO	TV Commentator
TERRY O'NEIL	Top Photographer	DON ARCHELL	Actor
WILLIAM FRANKLYN	"What's My Line"	JIMMY HILL	TV Commentator
JULIEN HOLLOWAY	TV, Films	GERRY YOUNG	"Coronation Street"
ALAN PRICE	Recording Star	DERYK UFTON	Ex-Charlton
PETER SHILLINGFORD	Film Director	JOHN RODEN	Actor
TONY CHARLES	Fashion Designer	TREVOR BROOKING	WEST HAM UTD. FC
KEN ADAM	Agent	RODNEY MARSH	MANCHESTER CITY FC
IAN LA FRENAIS		BOBBY MOORE	WEST HAM UTD. FC
NICK NEWMAN	Recording Manager	FRANK LAMPARD	WEST HAM UTD. FC

Match commentary by Ted Carson "Monty Python"
All the personalities will attend subject to commitments

Murder?

All hail to Au~~gustus~~ Archibald Von Gerda
The man who i~~nvented the perfect murder~~
~~Until that time nobody knew~~ Until that ~~time certain~~ magic day *FAR-OFF*
To kill,nobody knew the way
They8d hit each other with pillows filled
With feathers,but no one got killed
Theyd pour hot jam on each others head
And while some got sticky none got dead
~~Thax~~ They wept,they whimpered,~~there must be a way~~ Oi oi vay
To dead ~~someone, if someone said, there must be a way~~ each other ~~must be a way~~ *THERES NO WAY*
~~if we could it~~ But if we found it,aaah ~~theyd~~ chortle
Then we could prove we were i~~mmortal~~

~~But~~ *So* Archibald devised a plan
A way to kill his fellow man
I8ll try it on myself,he thought
And so a ~~heavy~~ book he went and bought
He hit himself upon the head
With his new book,but he didnt dead
He ~~merely raised a nasty bruise~~
~~(You may have tried to made him~~ Which didnt really ~~make good news~~

A~~haha~~ I8ll find a way,another angle
He thought,perhaps I8ll try to strangle
Myself with my bare hands. He tried
Strangly-wangly but he didnt died
He jumped into a ~~vat of custard~~ bowl of custard
He stuffed his nose with Colmans mustard
He ~~cut his throat with a slice of bread~~ *HE THREW HIMSELF ONTO HIS*
~~But alas and alack he didnt dead.~~ *BUT HE DIDNT DIED AND HE DIDNT DEAD* *FEATHER BED*

He jumped off a chair nearly two feet high
He d~~rowned~~ himself in a chocolate pie
~~He threw himself into the stinky skies~~
He threw himself into the loo *?*
But he wouldnt flush. What shall I do -
Wailed poor live Archibald Von Gerda
~~M~~ If I cant murder me,then who 6an I murder

Then fate took a hand as it often will
One day while busily trying to kill,
Himself by eating ~~the railwayside crusts of mouldy bread~~ *RANCID YAK*
He tr~~ipped~~ off his chair & ~~cracked his head.~~ *BROKE HIS BACK.*
The last words of Archibald Von Gerda
Were -~at last I have invented murder.

BUT
The ~~police~~ coroner ~~the~~ wasnt satisfied
And brought in a verdict of suicide.

TRAVELLING LIGHT

Recently I moved into my own head.
It's not a pretty neighbourhood
But on the whole you meet
A better class of people about this place.
Some nights I go out of my head
But most nights I stay in and read my mind.

I want to say this simply so that
You will not misunderstand.
Travelling light is a state of mind
Not a quantity of baggage.
There is nothing wrong with insanity,
It's just had some bad press.
Identity = Sanity.
It's the box you keep your ego in.
To be free = Insanity.

You can only see the dark by day
Because there is not enough light at night.
I carry myself around all day
From day to day
From place to place
But I am too heavy for me to carry.

But where else could I live
If I lighten my load?
Consider all that goes on inside your head,
Reconsider all that goes on outside your head.
Travel light.

EYE-GOR

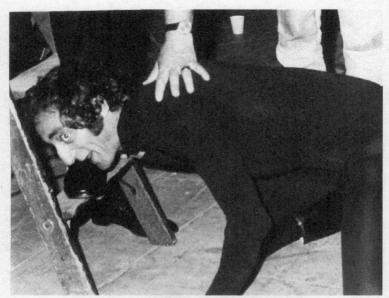

At our rather lavish abode, Lauretta would have a string quartet or small combo set up as we all had tea and eats and lay around enjoying the spoils of southern Californian culture.

Mel had pulled together a great cast and crew. The wardrobe lady was Dorothy Jeakins, and she and I really hit it off. I was scared silly: it was my first American film and entry into big-time filmmaking. Dorothy would calm me down during fittings by telling me great stories about working in the biz. She had won an Oscar many years before and had continued to do great work. She'd just come off the film *The Way We Were*, which my twin Robert Redford had been in. She told me I was just as handsome as him!

I became the only guy to appear in a horror film without make-up!

It wasn't a long shoot and we spent time in a small theatre in Santa Monica and had a blast with everyone involved. We would take breaks and walk for one block and be on the beach, not always the best place to be when sporting a heavy black cloak!

Like me, Teri Garr was new and we bonded a bit through our nerves and awe.

Peter Boyle had done quite a lot but this was his first big film, I think. Madeline Kahn and Cloris Leachman were seasoned pros and never missed a beat.

The house we had rented was as scary as the set created for the film. It had previously belonged to an actor called John Dall, whom we had seen in Hitchcock's *Rope*. He died in mysterious circumstances and was found on the floor of his bathroom with a massive head wound. Neither Lauretta nor I believed in ghosts and such, but the place scared Lauretta no end.

On the set I was doing my very first scene, a shot in which I knocked on a huge castle door three times. We rehearsed it a few times, for camera positions. When I did the first knock, the whole castle felt as if it was going to fall around me. At the very same moment a massive earthquake shook us and everyone was running for cover except me. I had never been in one before and thought it must be a prank to break in the new boy. I stood there during strong aftershocks until Mel screamed at me to get out of the way: he was sure I'd be killed, with stuff shaking and falling around us. When it finally calmed down a bit, I found a phone and called Lauretta, who was at the rented nightmare of a house. I asked her if she was OK and she said, 'Mart, this dead fucker is out to get me – there are things flying all over the place.' I don't think I've ever laughed as much in all of my life. Welcome to Shaky Town!

I had a great time with Mel who was constantly pestering me because I was doing all my own stunts. We shared a love of Yiddish humour and would cackle at each other all day.

I had never been on such a relaxed set – we all had so much fun. I tend to relax only when a show is over but this time I didn't want it to end.

Making films in those great studios, and locations like the small theatre in Santa Monica, was unlike any other experience. The tea ladies and gaffers loved what they were doing and knew as much about shooting a film as anyone. I was doing what I had dreamed of as kid, making a Hollywood film with big-time people. At any given moment you would turn around and a legend would be dropping by to say hi to someone we were working with, mostly Mel and Gene.

I had a really good relationship with Gene. He was a star but never acted like one. He would say, 'Everyone is a star to someone,' whenever somebody complimented him or talked about how famous he had become. He was the kindest man I had ever met. He insisted that all of the actors got paid the same. I'd never heard of such a thing. I felt I had a small role and in no way should I be paid the same as Peter or Madeline, never mind Gene himself. He reminded me of Tim Brooke-Taylor: when we acted in scenes together, we were not afraid to tap into our feminine side and be vulnerable. I decided that Igor should speak like an innocent kid and Gene liked that. I told Mel it would put more kids in seats because they would relate to me!

Mel reminded me of Spike: both would take something and make it funnier. Sometimes they could make something better by changing one word. In my first scene, where I meet Gene at a foggy railway station and introduce myself to him, I was told he would follow me down some stairs. I said jokingly, 'Walk this way,' using my short cane to insist rather than merely suggesting it. I did it to make Mel laugh because it was an old Yiddish joke. Gene played along, we got a few giggles and Mel loved it. We kept it. Gene told me afterwards that I'd better talk Mel out of it – we both thought it was a cheap joke and corny – but he would have none of it. When the film was first screened to an audience I was told that not only had the scene remained in but it had got a really big laugh. That's why Mel is great at what he does.

Friday nights were hangouts for cast and crew, family and friends. Mel would have it catered and there would always be fun things going on. It was the ideal way to meet new people in a new town.

POEM FOR MEL

As blue is to bluish
I am not Jew but Jewish
Which is something I ought to explain
For by strict definition,
You are Jew by volition
A religion from which I abstain.
So though to a critic
It may seem pedantic,
I'm not anti-Semitic
Merely anti-semantic.

Every project is a learning experience but with Mel and Gene I learned more than I had on anything I had done before. Both men stuck to their principles, and maybe because they were riding high on their previous successes, they didn't give in to pressure from other creative forces.

Mel insisted the movie should be shot in black-and-white and even threatened to walk when challenged about it. He was very easy to work with, and Gene didn't mind when dialogue was changed on the spot. Like most great directors, Mel inspires confidence in his choices. We all knew we were in good hands and that he would keep all the real monsters at bay. Even my roaming hump was initially a joke – one day I wore it on the other side to see if anyone would notice. Mel and Gene said that it should be part of the gag – what hump!

Gene had excellent timing and, like Rock Hudson or Steve McQueen, he could do more with his eyEs than most could do with their whole body. He kept it simple, and this was a marvel for me, being such a physical performer.

After I'd finished the film there was talk about us all working together again – Mel had an idea to use all of his comic heroes in a slapstick film. Gene had decided he wanted to direct a film of his own. Both had been planning this for a while.

When the film came out people were talking a lot about my part. I didn't see what all the fuss was about. I went on *The Johnny Carson Show* and he informed me that some were saying I'd be nominated for an Oscar. I thought this was daft. He asked what I was doing next. I told him I was on his show to promote the film but also to let people know I was available for work.

He thought I was joking but soon realised I was serious. I'd had no real offers and thought this was a good idea. My agents and manager were pissed off to say the least.

I accepted an offer to work in Canada for great money: I did two commercials and was open to any telly show that would have me. Having been wiped out with back taxes it was a time of uncertainty and I would always rather work than not. I was doing daft telly shows and cat-food commercials and I got that work myself! When I first met Mel he told me something that stuck with me. He said he saw immense talent in me and that I should protect it: I should only work with interesting people who were nice as well. He said I could forgive them for being uninteresting as long as they were nice! He was right, and I make it my mission, with Lauretta as my guide, to avoid any horrible fuckers.

UP YOURS, DARWIN

I'll be precise, I'll be succinct,
The dinosaur is not extinct
Whatever scientists say.

It's my belief
And I have found
The dinosaur is still around
He's just gone out to play.

So leave a saucer of milk out for
The poor forgotten dinosaur.

Acting came recently, but I have been a writer all of my life so I don't feel like I'm stuck if nobody says go. We should all be free agents: we should control our own destinies and get paid as much as we can get. My ambition is to be the world's richest socialist!

I was inspired by working with Mel and Gene, and knew that they wanted to work with me again but until the money is in the bank the bills pile high. The tax man indeed cameth! Gene was getting his act together fast for a film called *The Adventures of Sherlock Holmes' Smarter Brother*. I was to play the brother and before you could say, 'Another commercial', I had signed on as his willing and eager co-star, one Orville Stanley Slacker.

My agent had told me that the English papers were saying that, prior to *Young Frankenstein* opening in England, I was washed up and trying desperately to get work in the States. This has always been a sad trait of the British press: they have no grounds to base anything on but print it regardless and, sadly, people buy it.

I had a lovely lady come up to me on the set of *Sherlock*. A friend of one of the crew, she was there to have a look. She said she was so sorry things hadn't worked out for me! I could have pointed out that I was there doing another film with Gene, then going back to America to work with Mel Brooks again, and that I was in a film that was a hit in cinemas now, but why let her feel any better?

A strange thing happens when you're working on movies that doesn't so much happen in telly: you get thrown into this intense family working situation, rely on each other and thrive in it, and as soon as it ends you wake up the next day a bit depressed: your family have gone and, worse still, are off to climb another huge mountain and don't need you, never mind how pivotal you were to them.

Once Lauretta and I had finally worked out our differences with the British taxman, we put our Hampstead home up for sale and had no regrets, only good memories. England was over for me, at least for the foreseeable future.

I lost interest when Margaret Thatcher was elected to lead the Conservative Party. I had been reading about her for a while and thought she was a Fascist. Calling her a woman set the women's movement back years.

In America the Vietnam War was finally over and, though the economy was in a hole, there was a feeling of optimism.

In England everybody was hurting, inflation was at its highest ever and Thatcher and her crowd were using it to fuel their rise, much as Hitler used the German people to turn against minorities when the German economy was bad. I hated it all and couldn't wait to get out. I had no family left in England: my mum had moved to Spain after my dad died and any family home was gone.

Lauretta did all the business on getting our belongings together to be shipped to America. We now had money enough to buy our own home in LA.

I had received word from my agent that a few studios wanted to meet me and talk about doing some of my own films with me, so I could breathe again. As soon as we were back in LA I saw Gene about his project and right after that I met with Warner Brothers and Universal Studios executives about my vision for a future as a filmmaker.

Later that day Lauretta and I went home-hunting, which was draining, the agent was trying her best but we seemed to look at endless places we really didn't like. Lauretta had begun the search and narrowed down the candidates for me to dash around and see what there was. She didn't seem to like any of them but we had to find a home. We knew we wanted somewhere near the studios but it had to be surrounded by trees. We had all but given up when, on our way home, Lauretta spotted a house in the Canyon as we drove by. She asked the agent to stop, saying it was more like the kind of place we needed. I asked the agent to stay put in the car and I would go and see if I could buy it. She freaked out and told me that was not the way these things were done. She was still yapping when I was halfway up the drive.

I knocked, and a very nice lady came to the door. I said, 'Hello. My name is Marty Feldman and I would like to buy your house.'

She asked me to come in and explained that her husband had just died and she wanted to move. I told her I didn't need to see around it, just wanted to buy it from her and that she should just tell the agent how much.

Her husband turned out to have been the great actor Lee J. Cobb and they had raised their kids in that wonderful house. It sounds cold of me to barge in on her but she was very glad I'd shown up when I did. Lauretta and I were relieved too. In the end, we had a quick look around and it was much bigger than we needed but it felt like home from the first moment we sat in the kitchen.

That house became our social hub and we never wanted to leave. There were all sorts of rooms and a swimming pool, and I felt I could relax in many different places around the new gaff. All of the furniture that we'd loved in Hampstead just fitted in. The crazy fireplace that Peter Cook had given us – he'd spent far too much money on it – was put in the living room and I was happier than an old pig in his own sublime shit. I was writing like a madman – the house inspired me. Lauretta had us settled very fast and we soon had chums over on a regular basis.

When you come from a poor background the only experience you have of seeing how the other half live is through telly or in magazines. It's nothing like that: comfort is more than possessions. Just sitting in your favourite chair and reading a book is worth all the money in the world. When you make a chunk of money you still end up doing the same things most of the time. The seismic change is within.

Being brought up without the security of financial solvency can make the experience of becoming wealthy more enjoyable, especially in my case: I felt as though it might all revert back to park-bench living at any moment. We soon gathered a close-knit bunch of pals around us, like Stanley Dorfman, Ian McShane, Dick Clement, Ian La Frenais and Georgia Brown, and new pals like Harry Nilsson, and Van Dyke Parks, with his wife, Sally. Anne and Ted Levy, Spike and various Pythons visited us. It was great to meet friends from home who had also been displaced and were enjoying their new surroundings.

Dearest Gene,
In England I have a reputation for calling up directors and producers who've offered me a gig and convinced them that I'm wrong for the part offered me. I mention this in order to convince you that my argument which follows re Sherlock Holmes is based upon some twisted sense of personal integrity tempered with only a dash of greed. When you first told me about your Sherlock Holmes idea, I turned mental somersaults of glee at the notion of playing Slacker.

A. Because I'm dead right for the part.

B. Because I want to work with you.

C. Because we have a fine bunch of talented kids and my grandmother has a barn and I prefer movies to life, etc., etc.

But mainly because of A and B. I am right for the part and I do like you so. If I weren't right I would have told you immediately or alternatively you wouldn't have told me at all in the first place.

I understand your reservation about being thought of as being tied to me by some invisible umbilical cord, like Gabby Hayes to Roy Rogers, or Phil Silvers to everyone, but I don't think two films separated in release dates by about a year could be considered a marriage. A year by the way in which you will be employed in other Feldman-less ventures, and in which I at least will be employed.

Back to A, which I believe to be the first consideration. Am I right for the part?

Well, I've already told you I am, unless you want to make me a liar!

I remain yours obdurately,

Orville Slacker (yclept: Igor Feldman)

I was soon on my way to foggy London Town to be in Gene's film, which was shooting at Shepperton Studios. We got there in time for *Young Frankenstein* to be in cinemas and celebrated as a hit. The papers were proclaiming I was back in every way possible. How fickle the wind that blows upon our fair shores!

I was doing press for *Young Frankenstein* and *Sherlock* as soon as we landed.

Most commonly journalists asked me if I missed London terribly. I learned not to rub anyone's face in it, but I really wasn't missing it at all. Life was great where I was.

English interviews took on a different tone after I'd begun to make a name for myself in America. They would always try to get me to complain about Americans, which I never did. They followed up by trying to make me turn the bitter card on my homeland. They'd stop at nothing.

The other question I got asked was whether I was going to have kids and, if so, when and how many! You learn to let it go but I tried so hard to be honest with these people: that way I wouldn't have to remember the lie. But, really, what if we couldn't have kids and really wanted to? Such personal questions are ploys to put one on attack mode.

It rained and even snowed every day we were there. The cast members, like Madeline Kahn and Dom DeLuise, couldn't believe it. They went sightseeing and said they couldn't see anything!

Gene was the sole writer and had done great preparation for the shoot. He knew exactly what he wanted and worked very fast. He and I got on well. He only panicked a couple of times, which impressed me. Once he asked Mel to help him out and Mel, being the champ he is, calmed him down and told him to stick with it.

My part was good and, as in *Frankenstein*, I didn't have too much to do.

There was a lot of music in the picture – Gene had written it almost as an opera, with all sorts of old music-hall elements that were fun to return to. Madeline, Gene and I did some brave stuff together – we had already established a good rapport.

Funny films, like jokes, are all about timing, and a musical structure is a fantastic base to work with. I was learning to play drums properly now and had started to take lessons. I even spent time soberly with Keith Moon, whom I had become chums with, and tried to learn as much as I could from him.

We had some of England's best actors on the picture: Roy Kinnear, Trevor Howard and even Albert Finney. Albert and I got horribly drunk one night in a nearby pub with Spike and Peter Cook, whom I'd asked to join us. I suffered from the delights of it for days afterwards – my countrymen said Hollywood had dried me up and it had been their duty to dampen me back to reality.

Most of my close friends I could see in California, but it was worth poking my nose over the fence to check on friends like Graham Chapman and his chickens now and again. Overall the film was fun. It felt like a whirlwind because I kept as busy as I could in London, doing press, telly and anything else I was offered to make the time go faster: I was keen to get back to LA and do some writing. I felt the need for light and sun on my face.

Offers were coming in, but I was trying to focus on doing Mel's next film and get my head around a particular proposition from Universal, which involved doing my own thing – or things, even.

A note from

Gene Wilder
(The World's Greatest Lover) 10 March 1977

Dear Marty and Lauretta; thank you for your love. I use it every day.

Love, Gene

When we returned to LA from England we tried to lie low, but that lasted less than forty-eight hours. Between meetings and press I had little time to enjoy our new home. Mel had sent me a message, saying, 'Stay put and get ready to get silent.'

Acting was where it was at now for me. Even though I had been writing up a storm, there were no takers: making money to get out of a hole and finding a home proved to have been the right move.

On the first day of shooting Mel's *Silent Movie*, I met Sid Caesar, who was also in it, and said hello rather nervously. I asked how he was doing and he brightly replied, 'Earning and learning, son.' That was exactly where I was too, and it was great to be working with a legend who had been through it all.

It didn't take long on the set for the fun to start up. I became convinced the film would be rubbish because we were having so much. Mel was starring, as well as directing, and was great to work with because, not only was he a fan of silent movies, he understood the mechanics. I can't imagine what the studio's thoughts were when Mel told them he was going to do a silent picture with me and Dom DeLuise as his co-stars. He had brought in Barry Levinson and Rudy de Luca to co-write: both had worked on my *Comedy Machine* so I knew them and they knew I would go for anything I was asked to do.

The cast was fantastic. Anne Bancroft and Liza Minnelli were great, and there were cameos from all sorts of stars. I arrived each day to find Mel with a twinkle in his eyE, having talked Paul Newman into making an appearance. Burt Reynolds and all the biggest stars of the day showed up to take part or just hang out. It was amazing to see Mel talk people like James Caan into being in it. Caan was in preparation for his next film and needed to be in good shape. Mel convinced him to move his mobile workout trailer on to our set – he would pay for it – and told him he could take advantage of our nutritious catering. He bought it and was in the film before he knew it.

The great mime artist Marcel Marceau ended up in the picture too. I was thrilled to meet and work with him. We did a big benefit show around this time, and the stars appearing included Marcel, my old hero Danny Kaye and me.

This is the thing that happens in Hollywood: you never know what you're signing up for. *Silent Movie* became my most physical role by far because it was another short shoot. I packed into it every stunt gag I could and as a result ended up in poor shape. It also put a strain on my relationship with Mel: he'd known what he was getting into, but when he saw me falling around he didn't like it. I tried in vain to point out that, in my humble opinion, stuntmen are essential but I could fall funnier than any of them – I looked funny and he had me there to be funny. This is my instrument and it can be played only by its owner!

I was lucky to be in such good hands with Mel. He gave me great advice – he was very like my dad in many ways: they both loved their work and were happy to spend all the money they made by reinvesting it in their work. The one downside of the shoot was that I'd done severe damage to my back but tried not to let on. It would continue to haunt me and the pain never let up.

When *Silent Movie* came out a lot of people told me it was their favourite of everything I had done. So there it is. Not a perfect performance, but the movie was different from anything else that was around at the time.

When I wasn't shooting, I was at meetings with Universal Studios to see what they had in mind. I was offered a multi-picture deal with crazy money and they told me they felt we could do great things together. I kept calm and protective of my brand. I had come to them with the idea of pitching one of my script ideas. My manager told me to hold back and see what they said first.

Now I was sitting there and they already had contracts drawn up ready to do whatever I wanted to do.

I said I wanted to do a remake of *Beau Geste*, calling it *The Last Remake of Beau Geste*.

They loved the idea and informed me that they owned the original and it would be easy.

Here is a lesson to learn: be careful what you wish for. Not only did they not know I was kidding, but I was actually thinking of the wrong Foreign Legion film. The film I had in mind was called *The Four Feathers*, which had already been remade a few times. Ironically it was remade again the same year that my remake of my Foreign Legion film debuted. What a weird world I was entering.

You never do know! I was starting to learn the value of having a team on movie sets much as I did on my telly shows. Mel secured the services of actors and crew for both of the films I did with him, and it really cut down on time spent in pre-production. Getting to know you . . . The other outstanding thing Mel created was a sense of not knowing what each day would bring: I never knew which celebrity guest stars or visitors would come to the set, but also he would change things at the drop of a hat without freaking us out too much, which brought a great energy to the proceedings.

I made a note to copy that carry-on.

KOTO FLUTE

Koto Flute, keening,
Tiptoe into long unopened rooms,
Awaken the ancient Dung-gods
That are sleeping there to let the
Sun in,
Ting-a-ling,
I Ching.
Soma Solace,
Monkabird and Moonchance Beboptised.
Time ticks in your breath
Down corridors of memory where dreams lie,
Where is no silent resting place.

Now I was going on a brief holiday and then I was to move into my bungalow on the Universal lot to begin writing and production on my next project, *The Last Remake of Beau Geste*. I chose my good friend and constant performing partner from telly and our live show, Chris Allen, to write the screenplay with me. He was the perfect choice to work with. We had toyed with many film ideas before I was offered this, and here we were with a chance to knock it out and then introduce an original of our own. We had two scripts we loved but had to put them aside in order to get *Beau* in order.

Muhammad Ali is the greatest; David Frost would argue *he* is; Mel has openly told people that he himself is the funniest man alive. I have spent forty-odd years trying not to grow up and be defined, or proclaim myself, as the best or the worst at something.

Picasso once said, 'It took me seventy years to learn how to paint like a child, not childlike.'

Beau!

A different kind of love story.

THE LAST REMAKE OF BEAU GESTE

MARTY FELDMAN ANN-MARGRET MICHAEL YORK
PETER USTINOV and JAMES EARL JONES
"THE LAST REMAKE OF BEAU GESTE"
also starring TREVOR HOWARD · HENRY GIBSON · TERRY-THOMAS
Screenplay by MARTY FELDMAN & CHRIS ALLEN · Story by MARTY FELDMAN & SAM BOBRICK
Music by JOHN MORRIS · Directed by MARTY FELDMAN · Produced by WILLIAM S. GILMORE
Executive Producers HOWARD WEST and GEORGE SHAPIRO   PG PARENTAL GUIDANCE SUGGESTED
A UNIVERSAL PICTURE TECHNICOLOR

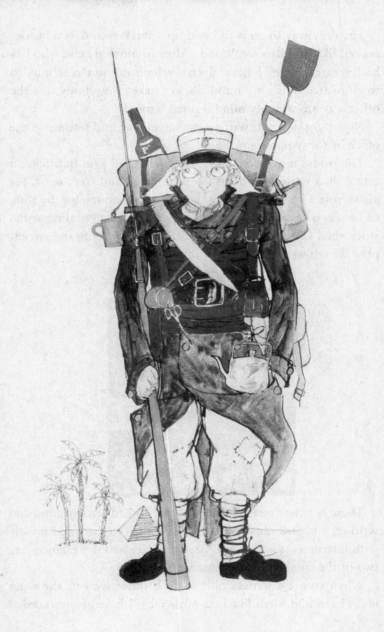

The only way to go is to build up a track record as a movie-maker, like Mel Brooks, Woody Allen or anybody else who has had a career at it. I have always valued my gut reactions to work-related stuff: my mind doesn't inform my body; it's the other way around. My mind is often wrong!

Now I got down to writing the screenplay and setting up the office in a very open way.

The studio introduced me to a bloke called Sam Bobrick, an established writer on shows like *Bewitched* and *Get Smart*. He also wrote a hit song for Elvis: he was good enough for the King so he was good enough for the pauper! We did an outline of the story, then Chris and I went into seclusion to write the screenplay. We felt we could knock it out fast.

There is a clear relationship between comedy, performing and writing, and jazz music, which is why I try to surround myself with instruments and records. Spontaneity and dry nuances are two of the common denominations.

When comedy writers talk to each other we riff, throwing ideas back and forth like jazz musicians. I have always needed this, whether with Barry or Chris, or a larger ensemble, as there was with *The Frost Report* or the *1948* shows. I thrive in these settings. I set up drums wherever I work.

I didn't want to burn out. I had just done three movies back to back and almost broken my back in the process. So the hours and such were liberal to start with. Being in Cary Grant's former bungalow and next to Hitchcock's home-from-home was considerably inspiring.

Lauretta surprised me with a great little car for my birthday. A blue dune buggy that, in its own sweet way, looked like me. My office at the studio was close by so she knew I couldn't get too crazy with it but I did give people a jump now and then. I'm not a great trumpet player and really try on the drums, but I'm a bloody awful driver.

I have so much adrenalin flowing through me that I flail around in my sleep like a crazy person. My car is just like me, a little package with a huge engine, and I often seem to arrive before it does. We are perfect for each other.

I wanted to hand the script in on time and, like a good whore, I can do it in any position. It was exciting and frustrating to be working on a studio lot.

Our bungalow was at first in a nice quiet spot but a few weeks later they lifted it up and moved it to another part of the grounds. The new location was right on the path of the tourist buses that would roll by all day long with people pointing at us. We closed the blinds but we could hear the tour guides on their speakers saying stuff about *Frankenstein*. Finally I could take no more and snapped. I set up a lemonade stand, charged way too much and hurled abuse Cockney-style at my customers, like a raving loony. I would ask them for their autographs, then wonder what they'd been in and if they knew they looked much bigger on telly.

The studio brass got wind of it and I was summoned, as expected. I explained that if tourists were allowed to come to my workplace and behave like idiots and the studio was to make money off them I should be permitted to do the same. They were very relieved when we handed the script in early and were only too happy to help with travel arrangements.

I was asked to present an award at the Oscars and did a gag that everyone in the room thought was funny but afterwards I had hate mail from people who thought I was disrespectful and bitter. I was presenting for a live-action short, and as the two people who worked on the thing came to collect their tin-pot trophies, I threw it on the ground and broke it in two, handed each a bit, said something silly and walked off. It was an obvious fake trophy and I got a giggle.

When we were shooting in Ireland I had a stranger come up to me and say, 'Well done in breaking that feckin' prize on telly. With half the world starving 'tis a disgrace.' I concur!

I was always wary of any authority, going back to my so-called teachers, so the studio brass were never able to get that close to the Beast.

I had read everything there was to read about Buster Keaton, his rise and fall, so I knew if it could happen to the Master it would surely afflict the pupil. So I started the relationship by leaving the studio bosses scratching their heads. The film was to be called *The Last Remake of Beau Geste* and I tried to have Robert Redford play my identical twin brother: I had mentioned my uncanny resemblance to him on telly and in print many times.

He declined and I got lucky with my new identical twin, Michael York. I was also lucky enough to con Ann-Margret, Peter Ustinov, Trevor Howard, Henry Gibson and many other great talents to join in on our way through Spain and Ireland. The locations were chosen because, at their most rural reaches, they resembled England and Morocco in 1906. We initially tried shooting at Shepperton, but England was too expensive and I was silently happy about it. I had spent the winter there doing Gene's film and felt that was enough. I still loved and missed many aspects of England, like the culture, the football, the arts and the pubs, but my fondness tended to be about the past.

Things came together fast on the production. Lauretta was an associate producer, which she had been before but now she was being paid and people listened. We were flying and enjoying every minute of it and I made certain it went to my head. Peter Boyle had told me on the set of *Young Frankenstein* that I would always be a star because I lived like one. When I asked him what he meant he said he'd noticed that I carried myself differently and did things differently and, as hard as I tried, I wasn't like the others. He said that he always felt ordinary, and even when people recognised him they asked what it was like to work with other people. I told him they just asked me repeatedly why I was incapable of having kids!

The film started off great and I tried to copy things from Mel, Gene and others I had worked with and admired. I tried to make the set a comfortable place for people to create. Lauretta helped immensely. She has always had a scary ability to know exactly what I'm thinking, no matter what kind of face I'm wearing, and she always tells me the truth.

I was stricken with an awful dose of chickenpox and had lumps all over my body. I woke up in the middle of the night and was convinced I was being attacked by a swarm of super-bugs, but Lauretta was lying beside me and had nothing. We went to the doctor and he told me I would be down for a while. Perfect timing, just like my drumming. Lauretta was my champion and got me through it without shutting things down.

There are vast amounts of this part of the story I don't remember, and maybe that's for the best. Some couples simply can't work together but we figured it out and, for me at least, it was easy.

I love you so much today,
Twice as much as I did yesterday
But only half as much as I will tomorrow
So at this rate you are getting a good deal.
Till then I'll love you anyway, baby.
All we have is each other.
What more could we want?

I am a dedicated manic-depressive. About every six months I slip into a black spell and Lauretta doesn't try to figure it out or cheer me up. She leaves me alone except when bringing me food or goodies and knows that I will be all right. I would never commit suicide for fear that I would be killing an innocent man.

We want to be Christ,
We want to be Jesus,
But nobody hears us
And nobody sees us,
God's gone away and he don't give a damn
So here I come
Whoever I am.
Stand back!

Working is essential for my type of personality. It has a cathartic effect on me. There is a lot of energy inside me that needs to get out. A lot of violence that I need to release. I have found swimming helps but obsessing over my work does the trick. It passes when I get my sleeves rolled up and charge into it head on.

Something that didn't pass, however, was the rain that stayed very much in the plains of Spain when we were there to shoot our desert scenes. We could have done *Noah's Ark* while we were there.

Ireland was lovely, as were its people. I hadn't been back since my days with Maurice and Mitch, and it seemed that time had stood still in many parts. We shot in the south and there were characters on every corner. This was the part of Ireland that Lauretta's family came from, mostly around the city of Cork.

We got really lucky in finding a young actor to play me as a younger man. Young Michael McConkey, who had never acted before, showed up at an audition and was perfect. We became chums and I would work with him again in a heartbeat. He never lost his free spirit and was game for anything. Truly a rare and wonderful find.

As is my wont, I hired as many chums as I could. I knew my honorary Irish pal Spike would join me if he was available, and I was able to recruit Hugh Griffith, whom I'd worked with on *The Walrus and the Carpenter*. Roland MacLeod, who had taught me so much as a writer came on board, Johnny Morris did the music and Jim Clark was to edit. Like Mel and the others, I found it easier to work with people I knew and had a rapport with. I was protective of the script we had written. I'm still primarily a writer – it's my trade and I'll need it to fall back on when the looks fade!

For my own performance I went with the decision to be more still and rely less on my eyEs to do the work. I like long shots, and keeping things still and more theatrical.

I felt I had overdone the crazy eyEs routine and, like Dolly Parton and her considerable assets, I decided to let the song do the work. I was also still sore from my *Silent Movie* antics. The shoot was still very demanding, what with the weather, various maladies and my back injury, which had worsened, leaving me feeling like a very old person. Returning to the warm embrace of our home in LA was as good a medicine as I could take. I was on all sorts of pills for my back that I had to stop taking because they were doing me no good. Swimming was what I needed, that and a bloody sledgehammer!

We got word from the studio that they were happy with what they had so far, were keen to get it out and gung-ho with all sorts of promotional tools. This was to be their only comedy of the summer and Jerry Henshaw, who had given it the go-ahead, was champing at the bit.

On a break from the Spanish rain the cast assembled for a very bizarre meet-the-press interview deal. Peter, Ann-Margret, Michael, Henry and I sat in a cold Spanish studio while a room at Universal Studios was packed full of journalists, about eighty of them, to fire all sorts of questions at us. We could hear but not see them. We were being filmed and they could see us. With the time delay, us being sober and them not so much, it was a fiasco. We hadn't even shot half of the film and we were asked all sorts of strange things and soon zoned out – Peter may have even passed out at one point.

Not a good idea to have the world's press quiz a cast about a film they hadn't finished and were starting to get fed up with because of the damp weather and delays. I was starting to think that the hands we were placed in were shaky at best.

We went home for a few weeks and I was informed that they wanted me to do press in Europe and beyond while the film was being edited. Again, suspicions arose. As the director I thought I should be where the picture was. They compromised and arranged to have film sent to me on various stops. The first stop was the Dorchester Hotel where I was set up for a few days to do interviews. Before I faced the press I got to see a pass of the film and thought my head was going to take leave of my body. I was angry with myself for letting this happen and disappointed to say the least with my friend Jim, who was editing their version of my film.

After many threats from managers and unions and whomever else I could use, it was decided that I could do my own cut. It was like driving a bus full of kids at full speed on ice, when you've never seen a bus before. Oh, and there's a huge pile of shit on the windscreen! I didn't have enough time to correct it all and in any case it was becoming obvious they wanted to go with their cut.

FIDO

I had a Hippopotamus, I bought him for a song.
They were two dollars fifty, on sale at Thrifty,
And at that price how could I go wrong?
It followed me home quite tamely, it stopped when I said, 'Heel.'
I thought, for that price this Hippo's quite nice,
Second-hand but still a very good deal.

When I got home I was to put Humpty back together again. A bad workman blames his tools and I had nobody to blame but myself. It wasn't like I'd come up the Thames in a bubble: I knew I was getting into the shark tank, just forgot all of my protective gear. It was essentially an average film, not horrible, not epic and nowhere in between. I didn't have time to do what was needed. They ended up using their edit, which, much to my surprise, people liked. I have never seen it. Jim Clark had been forced to do that cut, and include takes that were never supposed to be in the film. He was better than that, but the studio were stronger and he had aspirations to do his own thing, so a bit of relationship-building was going on. I knew I had to take it on the chin and move on, hoping the bruises would fade.

I knew that people would decide for themselves what they thought of it, and if it sucked it would be gone like a wet weekend. With my live show, I'd felt that if it didn't get enough laughs, I could get them in the post-show Q and A. No such luck with a film: I couldn't rush out after it and say sorry about the lighting, sound, story and all else. Some people liked it, others not so much, but it made the money the studio needed.

I felt I would have a better chance of making something I liked with an original idea.

Gene described working on *Young Frankenstein* as taking a small breath of Heaven each day. My experience on *Beau Geste* was like being dragged through Hell each day. I couldn't wait for it to end.

It was time to get away and find some fuel to ignite in myself some interest in my chosen profession. Lauretta and I were keen to lie low and, for the first time in a long while, live life. We told all business people we were heading out of town. We were excited to take short visits to Santa Barbara or other beach spots but were even more excited to stay put, enjoy our home and catch up with pals.

Many ideas were fixing themselves to the lining of my brain and I needed time to sort it out before it came out. That is exactly what all writers and performers who work with their own material need.

My first order of business was to see where my next step was going to be. Lauretta and I thought that, if I could get a decent advance on my next Universal film, find out if the bosses were into it and would leave me alone to make and FINISH it, then we could take our time and I could do a few other things too.

I had spoken to Anne Bancroft about doing a stage show that I would write based on the life of Dorothy Parker. Anne would be great in any role but I thought that I could write a good play about Dorothy's latter days holed up writing in the Volney Hotel in New York. She had become quite isolated and drank a lot, and the idea of her looking back appealed to me. I was thrilled when I read that she had left all her money to Martin Luther King Jr. I needed time to do this so it went on the back-burner.

I was offered a telly show of my own, either a one-off or a series, by the same network that had hidden *Comedy Machine* from the American public. All thoughts of *Beau Geste* were fading fast. Things were snowballing but, as we know, snowballs have a habit of rolling downhill so I had to be smart. Even though I was living my dream of writing, directing and acting in movies, I had a wife to support, and a pet piranha that I kept in the toilet, so the wisdom was not to rattle the studio cage but to forge ahead with my next original script.

ME, TALKING TO AN AMERICAN TV NETWORK EXECUTIVE ABOUT POSSIBLE GUESTS FOR MY SHOW

Me: How about Ray Charles?

Ex: He sweats.

Me: Ike and Tina Turner?

Ex: They sweat.

Me: I sweat.

Ex: You're a comic.

Me: (thinks) I see. I test my theory.

Me: How about Godfrey Cambridge?

Ex: He sweats.

Me: He's a comic.

Ex: Yeah, but he's . . .

(The Exec pauses, ostensibly to light his cigarette, but really to give himself time to substitute another word for 'black'.)

Me: He's black. He sweats but he's black?

(He smiles weakly. I know he is going to say he voted for McGovern.)

Ex: You don't understand. They don't like to see black people sweat.

Me: Is Jew sweat acceptable?

He knew I was putting him on, but irony is apparently as unacceptable as a black person's sweat!

True event, sadly. I'd had a black man and a small person on my English show and nobody cared. Land of the brave, home of the free?

Prepare the shark tank for Mr Feldman . . .

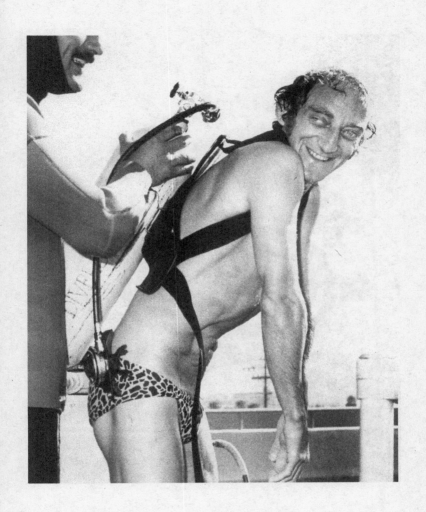

I continued to do telly performances. These shows really are the vehicle to get other projects going. I was on *The Flip Wilson Show* a couple of times and did some of the stuff from my first telly show, which got more attention than most films I was in. Carol Burnett, Bill Cosby – all those great talents had shows and were looking for nuts like me to come and pollinate every so often. Everywhere I went people would tell me they'd seen me on telly with Bill Cosby.

Humour evolves as we humans do. George Orwell said, 'All lives when viewed from within are a series of failures.' My failures were starting to mount. As a writer the same thing applies that happens with ageing: we tend to veer away from the use of adjectives and life becomes more about nouns and verbs, with an occasional adverb tossed in to remind you to check in with how you're getting on with yourself, from within.

It seems that all comedy comes from the same mainspring of the engine room, no matter what the superstructure is like.

The need to make people laugh and the craving for instant approval never leaves. Keeping myself from the negatives is a full-time number. I occasionally go back to the Fox set where we shot *Young Frankenstein* just to walk through the *Hello Dolly* set that is still standing there. It never fails to inspire me and keep a sliver of hope within. All the good times we had making our film there keep me going.

My dad used to say that they broke the mould when they made me, only I was still in it! The mould should have been for someone else – they should have taken a look and said, 'No, let's try again.' Luckily there's no such thing as a Marty Feldman type because nobody I have met looks like me. This enables me to write things that work for me. I was never good at doing upper-class or well-to-do folks in sketches, the odd, lower-class, naïve types are within my comfort zone. Still, on my next project I was determined to spread the old wings, albeit marginally. I could have my entire face fixed and play ageing leading roles!

There are lots of roles that are within my range as a comic actor. I would never try Hamlet – it would be ludicrous. I would sooner play one of the gravediggers than Polonius. I would like to play Estragon in *Waiting for Godot*: I understand him better than Vladimir, the other nihilist in the play, in the same way that I understand Laurel better than Hardy: Estragon is more pragmatic.

My goal on my next project was to create an interesting character for myself. Woody Allen would have been a typecast updated Wally Cox for ever if he hadn't written diverse roles for himself. I'm studying Woody and trying to figure out how I can apply myself through my writing to be more interesting than the one-dimensional slapstick figure that I had shaped.

Woody is a great and current light to follow.

While I was shooting in Ireland, I suffered the worst flu I had ever had and required intravenous fluids to stave off pneumonia. It was awful and I really thought I was going to topple off the perch. But I think the fever cleared my head, which was full of all sorts of ideas. When it had gone, the name Ambrose entered my life and wouldn't leave.

I had written a *Comedy Playhouse* script years earlier, called *Here I Come Whoever I Am*. The main character was played on telly by Bernard Cribbins and was called Ambrose Twombly. It was a short script that I liked, about a young bloke who really wants to fall in love. His character stayed with me and I felt it would be fun to see where he might have gone in his life. Did he fall in love, marry and have a bunch of kids? Or did he die in a war somewhere, never having had a relationship? Or perhaps he found another love in a monastery, the love of God?

The war idea didn't seem to have comic potential so I focused on the latter. I was determined to increase my fan base among boys of eleven or younger and old ladies so the role had to have a few dimensions. I'm not afraid to write something that doesn't have laughs. I feel I can still pull that off in performance but, as with my last film, I was feeling the need to be still and not rely on the uniqueness of my appearance.

First, though, my life had become full of excitement due to two hot new ladies who had moved in to live with me and the missus. They were two beautiful dogs we'd rescued from somewhere and I was following them around the house asking them nicely not to eat or poop on my work and life: that's the critics and studio bosses' job!

We had vowed not to get another animal after we'd lost our Yorkshire terrier Noko, so named because Lauretta loved the John Lennon song 'Oh Yoko' and had heard him sing it at a party in the late sixties. She loved the song and was convinced John was saying 'Oh, Noko'. That dog couldn't have been more different from the two new gals we named Lady and Sassy after our favourite singers, Billie Holiday and Sarah Vaughan. The girls are very needy and have to be told how much we love them. Noko wouldn't have noticed if we'd never come back to our house again.

We had secured the love and money from Universal and I actually felt good about it. I had the one thing I insisted on: they had given me complete control of cutting my next picture. I never signed a contract with these people, who were asking me to commit to five films: it was a handshake deal and I said I would come to work only if my films made money. I'm sure my managers saw it differently but for me that was the deal.

Much noise was made about my having a five-picture deal in America, especially in England where they would use it as a stick to whack me with if or when it did not work out. The interviews I was doing had already begun to feel like attacks, if only from the British press. When I was holed up in the Dorchester Hotel in London doing press for *Beau Geste*, most of the questions were about whether or not I was ever going to work with Mel or Gene again, and if there had been a falling-out. Another common theme was whether or not the films I had been in were dumbed down. The energy was moving away from the spirit of fun and adventure we had intended. Again there was talk that I was washed up and only in America to take the money. I didn't read any of these things: I was just gauging it all from journalists' questions. Lauretta did read everything and, ever my protector, let me know that my feelings were correct. Just as I said: when a child feels they're being persecuted, it's often for good reason. I told anyone who would listen that I had a one-picture deal and if that one didn't make cash I was in a no-picture deal!

By some weird series of events *Beau Geste* ended up making money, mostly from overseas but still and all. I didn't read any reviews but Lauretta did and kept them all. She had been doing this from the first time anyone wrote anything about me. I discovered a big chest full of the bloody things when we moved. My heart stood still. I had them all taken up to the attic and still have nightmares that I will awake and find my reviews suffocating me. Ironically the chest was the one I used in my *Monster* sketch!

For the first time in my life I was now in a position to relax and not fret because I wasn't working. I was still in the employ of Universal and their mighty bank account. I took it upon myself to write notes to all of the principal people who worked on *Beau Geste* saying that I was sorry our work hadn't turned out as we'd hoped and that it was only my fault, but I still had the keys and we would surely roar again. Trevor Howard and Henry Gibson sent very funny and kind notes back, and Peter Ustinov, who had offered great advice and was a huge help while we were filming, said, 'They ask you to bend over and while you are at it they kick you in the teeth.' Quite!

Still, I was already moving on. I've met a lot of people in my line of business who inspire me and make me feel I want to do better. My friend Harry Nilsson dragged me to many parties and gatherings. At one I was introduced to David Bowie. I'd thought for years that he was the bee's knees. He always reminded me physically of Peter Cook and in terms of originality.

MY HIPPO

I taught my Hippopotamus to beg and count to six,
To answer the phone and to play the Trombone
And other remarkable tricks.
I invited all my friends home to show what he was able.
When I said sit he frowned. He would sink to the ground
And let us all use his back as a table.

I still listened almost exclusively to jazz or classical music but I liked his work. He was an artist in every sense of the word. He was into mime and told me he was getting ready to do his first film, which turned out to be *The Man Who Fell to Earth* – I had been offered a role in it but couldn't do it because I was busy with other stuff.

We jokingly called ourselves the eyE to eyE brothers and decided it would be great to work together. My friend Stanley Dorfman had worked with him, and we thought the three of us could do a small weird film. I told him that I'd always wanted to do a stage play at the Roundhouse in London and that Beckett's *Waiting For Godot* was my dream. I'd hoped to do it with Spike but couldn't get it together because of scheduling. David was very excited and insisted we stay in touch. It was a very strange party, lots of drugs and people talking fast, and Harry, ever the goof, holding court.

David was from the same part of the world as me and we realised we had a lot more in common than dodgy eyEs. John Lennon was in town and I think the party was thrown in his honour but he never showed up. Harry Nilsson and John were very close and Harry would show him off in the best way: he knew that most people's lives would be better for having met him. John had that effect on people. He had become estranged from Yoko, and Lauretta would joke that she was ready to go off with him. She said the same thing about one of the Muppets so I wasn't too worried!

After a holiday I returned home, ready to write my next film. Once again I roped in Chris Allen. I thought about calling Barry Took to see if he was up for it but decided it best to start and then see if Chris and I needed help. Little did I know how long and arduous the process would be. We wound up writing five scripts over a two-year period. Lauretta did a great job getting me to focus on the task and keeping me away from other jobs. I was itching to do some live shows and still had offers coming in for other stuff too.

Chris and I had a great rapport and had worked together for many years. He had been onstage with me when we did our first live show in Australia. Writing can be tedious when you're working on a film idea. When you're writing an autobiography, a poem or a novel, that is the end product. Writing a script is only the first step in a lengthy process.

I had many ideas in my head and had written several different scripts. *The Queen and Me* is a story about a common bloke in love with the Queen of England. He is hired to drive her to various functions on a tour through America. She has become tired of her life and her marriage, and they take off on an adventure together. *The Great American Hero* follows the story of a comic-strip artist, who sets out to find the comic heroes of our youth. One by one he tracks them all down. They are living their lives outside the public eye. Dick Tracy is a gin-sodden wreck in his seventies, living in Arizona, and bemoans the death of simple values. Batman and Robin are living in a Bel Air mansion: Batman is an old queen in a wheelchair, superintended by his equally aged manservant, Robin, who wears an ill-fitting toupee and is constantly rerunning their old movies, like Gloria Swanson in *Sunset Boulevard*. He constantly complains that nobody needs or cares about comic-strip heroes any more. Marty, the comic-strip artist, assembles the heroes, including Superman, Mandrake the magician and the Lone Ranger. They form a Geriatric Dirty Dozen, setting out to fight their very last battle against IBM? General Motors? Universal Studios? Or is a computer the Force of Evil?

I put them all aside because Ambrose's voice was dominant in my head. I toyed with the idea of calling his story *Marty Feldman's First Second Movie* but eventually settled with *In God We Tru$t*.

> *Jesus cured, cared, the sun shone on the Holy Sea.*
> *He was the word, first last word, sent word for His sake, forsake,*
> *Across cross, criss-cross, having a here time,*
> *Wish you were wonderful.*

MY HIPPO

> *I sent my Hippo to the store to buy an ounce of mince.*
> *Well, I waited all day but I'm sorry to say I've waited ever since.*
> *Nobody's seen my Hippo since that faithfully day, and what's more*
> *The store's owner it is feared has disappeared And so too has the whole store.*
> *He kept the mice and rats out, I didn't need a trap.*
> *When I'd sit watching telly he would roll on his belly*
> *Or sometimes jump on to my lap.*
> *I call my Hippo Fido and he calls me Fido as well.*

Let's postulate a view of human nature, of history and, in particular, of politics that is pessimistic. Men never do good things unless necessity drives them to it. History is merely the record of their unchanging passions: we must reconcile ourselves to endless repetition rather than progress in human affairs. There is no higher destiny for man than to serve the state, and the state can only survive if its rulers reject all considerations of morality in the conduct of its affairs. Is this pessimistic view still tenable in the twentieth century? I believe that if we strip away the sanctimonious protestations of good-will we will see in this century the accuracy of my diagnosis. But why do we call it pessimistic? I tell the truth about humanity.

If a doctor tells you the blood circulates around the body, if Galileo tells you the Earth moves around the sun, are they called pessimistic? The truth is only pessimistic to those who live by myths. The Christian Church created the myth of divine grace: man is wicked but he is capable of redemption. When the myth began to die, we replaced it with the liberal myth of human goodness. It is this myth that prevents us seeing the world as it really is. Man is irredeemably wicked. His wicked-ness may be contained by the force and cunning of the ruler and modified by the precepts of religion, but it cannot be changed. Still, I recognise a role for religion even though I do not believe in God. I believe in the usefulness of the idea of God. Religion promotes virtue and unity, both of which contribute to the survival of the state, and the survival of the state is the only criterion by which we judge a ruler. In politics every action is judged by its effect. The question of good and evil does not arise. The ruler cannot allow morality or Christian ethics to influence his decisions in public affairs. The survival of the state is the only concern.

This may seem an anachronism in the modern world but the proliferation of states makes it evident.

The United Nations is a convenient forum for the pursuit of national interests under the cloak of international co-operation. No state allows its vital interests to be infringed unless it is too weak to prevent it.

That has always been the case and always will be. Now, the United Nations represents, especially perhaps for young people, a reflection of the old emphasis on nation states and a belief that the human race is one people. Men may turn to universalism when they tire of war, but it is unnatural.

The land of your birth is an accident of nature; to love your country is natural. But to speak of loving the whole of mankind is meaningless.

Men may be persuaded to subordinate their passions to increase the strength and unity of their country. To expect them to curtail them for the benefit of the human race is unrealistic. Questions of humanity are irrelevant to international politics. It may suit a government to appear to act for humanitarian reasons. Indeed, it is preferable that it should do so, but in reality it will be pursuing its own interests. The liberal myth blinds us to the truth. In the Second World War all states were motivated by self-interest. They did not fight because they opposed racism and oppression but because their vital interests were threatened. Similarly, no state today opposes apartheid unless it serves its policy to do so.

Rulers condemn or condone oppression as their own interests dictate. This realism in international affairs is more blatant than ever before, which is why rulers are at such pains to disguise their policy behind ideals – freedom, equality, tolerance and human rights – that blur the edge of national identity. Men will tire of peace as they have tired of war. The cycle will continue. The cast and props may be different but the plot will always be the same because man's passions cannot change. We claim progress, but is it progress if a cannibal uses a knife and fork? Has his nature changed? The Christian and liberal myths still haunt civilisation. Man's wickedness is for all time, without change and without redemption.

Yet, despite this, a few men and women live unselfish lives. It is an act of defiance. They feel compelled to deny a truth they cannot bear to contemplate. These are just a few notes on the human condition, which affect the attitude of my next film and, believe me, jokes are much funnier. Maybe there is a bridge between the two. Enter Ambrose!

Harry Nilsson and I were playing with the idea of the film being a musical. Harry had always been a reluctant performer and was keen to do more filmed musical adventures. A couple of years before, a group of us, including Harry, Van Dyke Parks, Keith Moon and me, were trying to come up with the idea of doing a small theatre musical that we had called *Good for God* after an older song that Harry was revamping. Even Ringo Starr, who always seemed to be busy, wanted to participate and shared our enthusiasm. I was in a writing frenzy and Harry was too. We loved Tom Lehrer and Randy Newman, both of whom had been guests on my telly show, and used them now as the standard of quality. The vast majority of these ideas were fuelled by various substances, but Harry and I became very serious. Sadly, I had become almost as big a drinker as Harry, who was already one of the heavyweight champions at it.

GOOD FOR GOD

I bet he's got a very hard job.
I'm awfully glad I'm here to say
He made it possible for me to be here to say
Good for God.

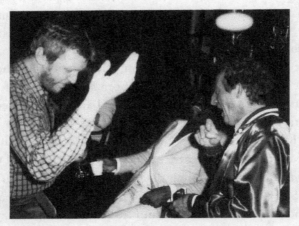

With Harry and Billy Henderson at home

The idea slowly redirected itself into a movie and we decided that it could have a musical quality but not be a musical in the traditional sense. The film was to expose the impossibility of practising pure Christianity as taught by Christ. I am a great believer in the message of Christ's teachings and think of him as an early Marxist. But is it really possible to live by his teachings today? Would Billy Graham give away his riches? Those who see the Bible as an allegory I expect do not object but anything that rocks the boat will cause upset, especially when 'written by Marty Feldman' appears on the screen. The last name may be an obstacle! Monk-meets-hooker was the selling point – boy-meets-girl movies are always a hit. I researched the whole manifestation of commercialised religion, from Billy Sunday and Aimee Semple McPherson to Oral Roberts, Marjoe Gortner and Billy Graham. Nothing I made up in my story was as outrageous as that which already existed and bested it from the television evangelists. Harry and Lauretta would watch stuff with me but eventually would gravitate to another room because it got too depressing for them. I was glued. This phenomenon does not exist outside America, and Los Angeles was a hotbed for revivalists, evangelists, occultists, phrenologists, fringe gurus and more. Just try to walk three blocks on Hollywood Boulevard and see if L. Ron Hubbard's crowd don't try to invade your life. I was more interested in the evangelists because they were representing Christ and were claiming to bring his word to us directly. I was not attacking religion, and that was to be clear, but I was aiming to take on the rip-off fundraising involved in it. Not great fodder for a slapstick fable but it overtook me. I wrote Brother Ambrose to be simple, innocent and childlike but not retarded. I suspect that Jesus Christ was more of this personality-type than his sales representatives who roamed the Earth a couple of thousand years after his life was over. Two of the studio blokes we were dealing with, Ned Tanen and Thom Mount, seemed to be well into it so it wasn't like I was trying to fuck them over. I hope that, no matter what obstacles present themselves in my life, I will always see comedy with a childlike vision.

I still love writing.

It is who I am, and has been a constant outlet for all of my disorders. Mental exercises are as important as physical ones and pushing our minds is essential, trying to learn as we grow.

I was more disciplined than I had ever been, not taking on other jobs, stepping out to live life yet not letting the ball drop. Our house had now become a home, like we had in Hampstead, and I was finding it very nice to stay still, which took a while to get used to. I am lucky to be paid for doing what I enjoy. I didn't start off with the aim of making money, but I would be writing even if I wasn't being paid at all. Still, it's awfully nice – I can afford goodies now! It's easier to write and not panic about working when you have a few bob in the bank. Money insulates you, buys you time and the freedom to explore yourself and your relationships to other people.

HAIL TO PONTIUS KAAK, FATHER OF THE MODERN DOORKNOB

Before the doorknob was invented people's doors got badly dented

*As they'd hang from inside and holler and shout, oh, tell us how
will we ever get out?*
They sighed
*Behind each blank and knobless door, huddled in hundreds upon
the floor.*

*They'd weep and they'd wail at their terrible doom, and curse the
cruel God who invented the room*
'S inside.
*But science, without which they'd reckoned, was speeding to their
aid that second,*
*As day and night at his lonely job Toiled Dr Kaak to invent the
Knob.*
He tried.

*His colleagues scoffed, he's off his head, it's heresy, God strike him
dead.*
*He's a communist pervert, they muttered, by God, a doorknob,
how terribly sad,*
They'd chide.
*But noble Kaak just slaved away convinced that soon would come
the day*

When he would to the whole world prove that people in rooms
would be able to move
Outside.

One night, he leaped from his lonely bed, an idea rang inside his
head.
It went tingley-ingly-ping! I have thought, he thought, of just the
thing
Untried.

Such are great moments to men of such vision, an inspiration, a
decision.
Suppose it turned? That'd do the job — and he rapidly sketched a
crude doorknob.
With pride

He ran to tell the people who were huddled still inside the room.
But woe, alas, poor Dr Kaak, excited, had a heart attack
and cried,

Don't worry, good people, in your room, I've come to save you
from your doom.
As soon as I'm in, you can all get out, But before he could open
the door, with a shout,
He died.

Each night, exhausted, he'd wake and sob, My kingdom for the
perfect Knob.
But should it push or pull or what? His fevered brain could really
not
Decide.

I never considered anybody else to play God but Richard Pryor. God apparently made man in his own image and that image is human and Richard is the most human of human beings I have ever met. All the pain and vulnerability are there but mostly there is a remarkable kindness and likeability. We went to every show in which he was performing in the Los Angeles area and he never once failed to make us laugh. When I approached him about the film, he really thought I was taking the piss, but the idea of playing God eventually seemed exactly the right idea to him too.

It took me a while to find the perfect person to play my evangelist and soon it became clear that Andy Kaufman was the man to play Armageddon T. Thunderbird. We had seen him perform at various venues and he had never failed to amaze us and everybody else.

Soon enough it all came together, and we had my friend Peter Boyle and the lovely Louise Lasser on board too. The studio were supportive and left us alone. The job of directing can be fun – I have described it as 'Dr Jekyll writes and Mr Hyde directs.' When I'm trying to protect the script, I stop and ask the good doctor if we're doing justice to his writing. I also try to have at least one cast member who is more experienced than I and, like dear Spike, can see things from a slant that is not the same as mine but compatible.

LETTER FROM SPIKE

Hello you and her

I see you bought the Queen's knickers, I hope you are keeping them fresh for my next visit to them shores, we can all go a-camping in them.

I am sending you a cutting which shows that your art is being refurbished on the wireless.

I was beginning to think you might have a writing letters hang-up but relieved to find you are still at it! I am glad you are making the best of it there, there are lots of wonderful things and lots of bloody awful things too. I hope you are doing alright with your entertainment.

I myself am off comedy at the moment, especially the TV variety, you know how you can write something funny that you know to be funny and it comes out unfunny. This part tends to leave me very depressed so I have gone sideways and am now writing music again. I used to write songs and did arrangements for the band in the army which we played against the Germans' band in action, and we always came off in a better key!

I am about to do some more recording with George Martin again after so many years and we are both looking forward to it.

I am getting all the usual brush-offs from the big boys but I will make it as a composer.

My love to you both, and more to her for being so unnaturally pretty!

Love, light and peace from Spike

PS Of course you will write and tell me how the premiere goes – good luck on that day.

PSS Remember, it only happens all the time.

I have also learned that directing a movie is easier than I thought it would be. As with most professions, there is a handful of truly great directors working in film today. There are several good ones, as with painters or architects. You either have it or you don't. Genius lives and greatness visits. I'm honoured with each visit. But I have yet to make a great film.

I have figured out how all the gear works and how to be nice with the talent when wrangling them all to work. I have invited other creative people to the set to see if they could add anything to the mix.

LETTER FROM JOHN LANDIS

4-17-79

Marty,

Leaving your set this afternoon, your prop man handed me a Buster Keaton pin.

Animal House was shot in Eugene, Oregon. The parade sequence we filmed in a small town 20 miles away called Cottage Grove. While shooting the big crowd stuff an old woman told me that this was the 2nd film she had been in. The first turned out to be *The General* which Keaton filmed there 50 years ago!

Now you're on the back lot of W. C. Fields, Abbott and Costello, Cary Grant and on and on.

Make a wonderful movie. Have a wonderful time.

John!

This is what keeps us strong against the commercial leanings of our landlords! John and Martin Scorsese, Woody Allen and Francis Ford Coppola are just a few who know their place in the order of things and tracing their steps is exhilarating to say the very least.

Still, at the age of forty-eight I am learning what Keaton mastered at the age of four! Talking to John Landis or Martin Scorsese about Jerry Lewis and the pioneers who are still with us, or gone but never forgotten, is a class you can never find in school. Like when I was helping Judi Dench, the great actress, find a house when we were living in Hampstead. Spending a day with that woman, whom I barely knew, as she navigated through her life, taught me more about the mind of a woman than reading any book!

I have always tried to use what I have learned or imagined and be eternally pragmatic.

In Hollywood they treat failure as a contagious disease: they don't linger for fear of catching it. All writers and directors working today know that we are only as successful as the takings from our last film. Years ago I was asked in an interview while rehearsing at Dallas Brooks Hall for our live tour, if the thought of failing gets in my way. I answered that what I endured in music hall and Margate's Dreamland had been enough for me to develop the thickest of skins. Having said that, I have since learned that failing on a grand scale in Hollywood is very difficult to deal with. Comics tend to exploit their own deficiencies and hang-ups, while writers are genetically tense, perhaps because they can't physically release their baggage. Both groups are an insecure lot because they need approval, need to be loved and hear that love through laughs or applause. Most are shy. To be in comedy is akin to being paid to parade one's neurosis. With my earnings from these parades, I would be a charlatan if I said

I didn't want them, but that doesn't mean I wouldn't want to see society change and distribute the dough in equal shares. It would be ideal not to need money at all, as naïve as that sounds. There are things I carry with me in my head at all times, not memory, more stamps that I check in on. I remember talking to Dick Lester, who had worked with Buster Keaton on the last picture Keaton ever did. Dick described how bad he had felt for Buster: nobody on the set of that film knew who he was and were quite disrespectful towards him. I know how great he was, and I am painfully aware of how it ended. I met his widow, Eleanor, who was so kind and still in love with him. I couldn't help but cry in her company. Lauretta bonded with her too, as I'd imagined she would: two strong women who spent their lives with men who never grew up! Eleanor gave me one of Buster's hats and I immediately stained it with tears.

Ironically I feel that my career is only gathering steam. Lauretta reminds me that I'm a novice on this side of the Pond and that I shouldn't be so hard on myself in what is a business, when all is said and done. I still feel I can make a profitable film but I must look to more independent avenues. People like Robert Altman can do it in their sleep while others chase themselves around trying to find the code. I am not a director because I am a writer and actor, and directing is not how I plan my working life. For *In God We Tru$t* I pulled together the same team as I had worked with on my last film.

One day I woke up to find that a few films were in production or about to be released with God as the subject. This was a drag because I had gone out of my way to try something different, but so, too, had Dudley Moore, the Pythons and Peter Sellers. Still, I got up and got on with it. I had a lingering feeling that this would be my final film with Universal and we decided to enjoy making it as much as we could. It was an easy shoot and suddenly it was ready to go. I was subjected to all sorts of test screenings, and most audiences found the film good but not that funny. There is only so much you can do in post-production – add a laugh track?

It soon became apparent that the boys at the studio were not going to promote it as we'd hoped.

Go on my son!

The political climate had changed and this silly person Ronald Reagan, a dodgy actor if ever there was one, landed the biggest acting gig of all, becoming President of the United States of America. He ran on a platform of having God on his side and seemed hellbent on making God his vice. Separation of church and state was thrown out of the window!

I was hanging out with Harry Nilsson on his birthday, watching Reagan campaign on telly, when the phone rang. It was John Lennon, calling to wish Harry a happy birthday. Harry told John about my film and how excited he was that it was coming out. John asked to speak to me, and was so funny, quoting dialogue from my old shows. He said he drove Yoko (they were together again) crazy every time they went somewhere by screaming, 'Wait for me, wait for me,' from one of my sketches. He talked about making music after a long time away from the studio and offered me advice on being a foreigner and challenging God in America. I had forgotten about his bigger-than-Jesus caper but he became very serious: 'Be careful, Mart. They're not like us, you know. Most of them are, but Reagan's crowd we are not.' When the poor soul was shot we, like everyone else, were shattered – he was bigger than Jesus for many of us. Poor Harry went to pieces and has never been the same since.

We were having a party at our house when the call came. Harry arrived shortly after and crawled onto the couch like a child. We took care of him as best we could.

John was not the only one who warned me. Richard Pryor took the role on the condition that he wouldn't be involved in flogging the picture. He would constantly say, 'All right, Mart, let's see if we can get this crowd to give up their pie because a Jew and a black are applying pressure!'

I was lucky to have such a great cast and crew who made my job easy. I was resigned to the fact that the film wouldn't be a smash hit but I still had hopes.

I had a call from Jim Henson who asked me to host one of his *Muppet Show* episodes. I was so excited because I was a huge fan. He and I had a lot in common in terms of influences. He liked me and I liked him. I wanted to present him with a script idea I had called *Spivs*, which I thought would be a great vehicle for us both. Jim was based in England so, as Lauretta had some gynaecological issues and wanted to see her doctor in London, we flew over. Lauretta's condition turned out to be worse than I'd thought – she hadn't wanted to tell me for fear of worrying me. As if I were a stranger to worry! She needed major surgery and I tried hard not to show that I was freaked out. She spent a week in hospital and I don't think I've ever cried as much in my life. It was the first time for years that I'd been on a set without her beside me, which was very odd. I asked Jim if I could use her name in the opening sequence and he agreed.

When Lauretta had recovered, we decided to take a holiday before the film was released in America. Years before, I was being tortured by Keith Moon to help him get a film about pirates together. After he died, my old pal Graham Chapman took up the battle and secured the dosh to put it together. I knew he would ask me to do it. Graham was moving to America with his boyfriend and adopted son. We were thrilled because he was family to us.

Me and Graham

Many years before this we were all hanging out at the bar in the BBC and, out of the blue, Lauretta told me she thought Graham was gay. I told her she was, too, in sarcastic response. This was long before Graham came out. He met his boyfriend, David, a really lovely bloke, while we were all on holiday in Ibiza shortly before we did *At Last the 1948 Show*. One afternoon Graham arrived at our house, as he often did, and asked Lauretta and me to sit at the table because he had something to tell us. We couldn't wait for him to get it out and laughed when he realised that telling us he was gay was like telling us he was tall. He said he thought that Lauretta knew and that was why he loved being with her. He had been seeing a bird before this and needed to clear things up a bit.

Now he was asking me to join him in his pirate adventure. He had already enlisted John Cleese, Spike Milligan, Eric Idle, Cheech and Chong, and was pretty sure David Bowie was on board too. I was in, but mostly because I would do anything for Graham and John because they had given me a start. I was happy to be a hired actor and took on a few jobs while we were in London. *The Muppet Show* was the one thing everyone talked to me about, and it was a great diversion from the failure of my last film.

I visited some family in London and drove Lauretta a bit nuts with talk of maybe moving back for a while because I was missing the work on telly. I did a show in Los Angeles called *Fridays* with a bunch of talented people but English telly is more my game. Anyway, once I'd been in London for a while, I realised again that England was no longer my home and it was skidmarks at the airport. I had become very unsettled after Lauretta had had her operation – perhaps it was the fear of losing her, an unbearable thought.

Before the film opened, I'd been even more selfishly unsettled. One morning, sitting at our kitchen table drinking tea and reading the paper, I blurted out that I thought we should be free to have sex with other people, that marriage and monogamy were antiquated traditions. I said that the government should set up taxable sex stations that people could nip into when they were going a bit crazy – think of how few sex offenders there would be. Lauretta, my long-suffering partner, got up and went to the other side of the house. She reappeared moments later with a bagful of my stuff and told me to get out and go fuck whoever I wanted. I tried pleading with her but in vain. As I drove off, not knowing where to go or what to do, I couldn't believe I had said such an insensitive thing. I was out of the house before I had time to grasp the depth of my blunder.

She wouldn't answer the phone. Days and weeks dragged on. I went to a hotel, but that freaked me out, and I ended up driving a great distance to stay with John Cleese, who was not only a good friend but also no stranger to love and flux. After a while he begged Lauretta to take me back because he couldn't bear it any more. Another debt owed to John. I was such a fucking idiot and learned from my mistakes. I had freaked out before badgering her about kids and whether or not we should have them.

When I got home I wanted to tell her about all my insecurities and fears over her health but she took me by the hand and told me to shut up and we went to our bedroom and closed the door. I cry when I think about how much I love her. Even as I write this she is in the other room keeping my life together. We decided that I wouldn't talk any more about death, which apparently I had been doing, and that we would enjoy our lives together more than ever. Work offers were coming in but I had to see how the film would do.

We finally premièred it with all of our friends gathered. It was a horrible event. Nobody laughed, and after about twenty minutes I ran out of the place and got completely smashed, drinking vodka at the Baked Potato, a jazz venue we frequented. I drank and drank as the band played some awful fusion shit but even that sounded better than the silence of the cinema. I passed out at or near the bar and woke up the next day in a nearby hospital. I had been taking prescription drugs for my back problem, which had worsened. I kept putting off the notion of surgery, which had always terrified me. It appeared now that I had three fused vertebrae, hence the horrendous daily pain. Now I was extremely numb, on my back, in a hospital bed accompanied by a drip filled with the right stuff!

When I woke up, Lauretta greeted me, calling me a silly sod. She had spent the night by my side and was worried sick. When I came round, she told me that everybody had seemed to like the film and thought it was good but not laugh-out-loud funny. She also said none of it mattered because Universal had already thrown in the towel and weren't going to push it. We thought that a decent publicist could create some adverse publicity.

Maybe a suicide attempt could do wonders for my career. I was actually starting to fancy the idea of disappearing altogether and letting people think I was dead. No such luck!

The bloke in the bed beside me was extremely annoying, and insisted on chatting with me as soon as Lauretta or anyone else left me. He had been admitted to this private hospital, which was supposed to be only for loony performers like me, because he had passed out in front of the door and they'd had to take him in. It turned out that he worked for the *National Enquirer* and was getting all of my details either from me or from my nurse. At least he got the story straight!

I don't want people to cheer me, but neither do I want them to throw bricks at me. I want them to know I'm here and trying. A healthy ego is necessary and very important. Without it, there would be little or no art, music, books or films. Ego is a Freudian term. It hangs people up, as it did its creator. He didn't have a psychiatrist because he invented the bastards, and it isn't the damage he has done that causes trouble but the damage done in his name, like Christ before him. And the effects are indeterminable. As Freud would say, 'I postulate.'

After I got out of hospital, I drove to the Universal lot very early one morning and, before anyone could say a word, I packed up my office, put the whole bloody lot in my car and vowed never to return, not that I had a choice at that point. I aspire to be here today, more so tomorrow and far gone in between.

I'd thought I was prepared for this but I felt awful for Lauretta and all the others who had put so much work into the film. Once again, I was embarrassed beyond belief.

It took me a while to get out of the funk from this one. And now I am studio loose and fancy free!

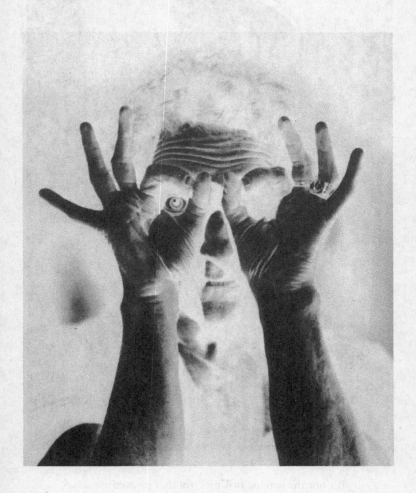

It's not the leaving of Universal that grieves me ...!

with the holes in the elbows. His toes wriggled sensuously inside his bedroom slippers.

'This is very pleasant, Galahad,' he said, and Gally endorsed the sentiment.

'I was thinking the same thing, Clarence. No Connie, no Dunstable. Peace, perfect peace with loved ones far away, as one might say. I'm sorry I'm leaving.'

'You must, I suppose?'

'I doubt if the marriage would be legal without me.'

'Someone you know is being married?'

'My godson.'

'I've never met him, have I?'

'Certainly you have. The chap who falls downstairs.'

'Ah yes. Who is he marrying?'

'Linda Gilpin.'

'Who is Linda Gilpin?'

'The girl who kisses him after he's fallen downstairs. I am to be Johnny's best man.'

'Who—'

'Yes, I see I'm confusing you, Clarence. Johnny and my godson are one and the same. All straight now?'

'Perfectly, perfectly. Your godson Johnny is marrying Linda Gilpin.'

'You put it in a nutshell. And I have to be there when the firing squad assembles. Furthermore, Trout and Vanessa Polk insist on me dining with them before they go off on their honeymoon.'

'Who is Trout?'

'The chap who has married Vanessa Polk.'

'Who is Vanessa Polk?'

'The girl who has married Trout. They've both married

each other, and they're going for the honeymoon to Nassau.'

'That's where the Falls are, isn't it? People go over them in barrels, which is a thing I don't suppose many young couples would care to do. But no doubt Mr. and Mrs. Trout will find some other way of passing the time. Vanessa Polk, did you say? Wasn't she staying here?'

'That's right, and so was Trout.'

'I thought the names were familiar. Nice girl. Very sound on pigs. I hope she will be very happy.'

'I'm sure she will.'

'And I hope your godson will be very happy.'

'Have no uneasiness about that. He loves his popsy.'

'I thought you said her name was Linda.'

'Popsy is the generic term. By the way, did Connie confide in you much while she was here?'

'Not very much.'

'Then you probably don't know that serious obstacles had to be surmounted before the Johnny-Linda Gilpin merger could be put through. It was touch and go for quite a time. Snags arose. Tricky corners had to be rounded. It was only at long last that they were given the green light. But all that's over now. It makes me feel as if I were sitting in at the end of a play, one of those charming delicate things the French do so well. You know the sort of thing I mean—lightly sentimental, the smile following the tear. I am having my dinner. The storm is over, there is sunlight in my heart. I have a glass of wine and sit thinking of what has passed. And now we want something to bring down the curtain. A toast is indicated. Let us drink to the Pelican Club, under whose gentle tuition I learned to keep cool, stiffen the upper lip and always think a shade quicker than the next man. To the Pelican Club,' said Gally, raising his glass.

'To the Pelican Club,' said Lord Emsworth, raising his. 'What is the Pelican Club, Galahad?'

'God bless you, Clarence,' said Gally. 'Have some more roly-poly pudding.'

P. G. Wodehouse

IN ARROW BOOKS

If you have enjoyed Blandings, you'll love Jeeves and Wooster

FROM

Aunts Aren't Gentlemen

My attention was drawn to the spots on my chest when I was in my bath, singing, if I remember rightly, the Toreador song from the opera *Carmen*. They were pink in colour, rather like the first faint flush of dawn, and I viewed them with concern. I am not a fussy man, but I do object to being freckled like a pard, as I once heard Jeeves describe it, a pard, I take it, being something in the order of one of those dogs beginning with d.

'Jeeves,' I said at the breakfast table, 'I've got spots on my chest.'

'Indeed, sir?'

'Pink.'

'Indeed, sir?'

'I don't like them.'

'A very understandable prejudice, sir. Might I enquire if they itch?'

'Sort of.'

'I would not advocate scratching them.'

'I disagree with you. You have to take a firm line with spots. Remember what the poet said.'

'Sir?'

'The poet Ogden Nash. The poem he wrote defending the practice of scratching. Who was Barbara Frietchie, Jeeves?'

'A lady of some prominence in the American war between the States, sir.'

'A woman of strong character? One you could rely on?'

'So I have always understood, sir.'

'Well, here's what the poet Nash wrote. "I'm greatly attached to Barbara Frietchie. I'll bet she scratched when she was itchy." But I shall not be content with scratching. I shall place myself in the hands of a competent doctor.'

'A very prudent decision, sir.'

The trouble was that, except for measles when I was just starting out, I've always been so fit that I didn't know any doctors. Then I remembered that my American pal, Tipton Plimsoll, with whom I had been dining last night to celebrate his betrothal to Veronica, only daughter of Colonel and Lady Hermione Wedge of Blandings Castle, Shropshire, had mentioned one who had once done him a bit of good. I went to the telephone to get his name and address.

Tipton did not answer my ring immediately, and when he did it was to reproach me for waking him at daybreak. But after he had got this off his chest and I had turned the conversation to mine he was most helpful. It was with the information I wanted that I returned to Jeeves.

'I've just been talking to Mr Plimsoll, Jeeves, and everything is straight now. He bids me lose no time in establishing contact with a medico of the name of E. Jimpson Murgatroyd. He says if I want a sunny practitioner who will prod me in the ribs with his stethoscope and tell me an anecdote about two Irishmen named Pat and Mike and then another about two Scotsmen named Mac and Sandy, E. Jimpson is not my man, but if what I'm after is someone to cure my spots, he unquestionably is, as he knows his spots from A to Z and has been treating them since he was so high. It seems that Tipton had the same trouble not long ago and Murgatroyd fixed him up in no time. So while I am getting out of these clothes into something more spectacular will you give him a buzz and make an appointment.'

When I had doffed the sweater and flannels in which I had breakfasted, Jeeves informed me that E. Jimpson could see me at eleven, and I thanked him and asked him to tell the garage to send the car round at ten-forty-five.

'Somewhat earlier than that, sir,' he said, 'if I might make the suggestion. The traffic. Would it not be better to take a cab?'

'No, and I'll tell you why. After I've seen the doc, I thought I might drive down to Brighton and get a spot of sea air. I don't suppose the traffic will be any worse than usual, will it?'

'I fear so, sir. A protest march is taking place this morning.'

'What, again? They seem to have them every hour on the hour these days, don't they?'

'They are certainly not infrequent, sir.'

'Any idea what they're protesting about?'

'I could not say, sir. It might be one thing or it might be another. Men are suspicious, prone to discontent. Subjects still loathe the present Government.'

'The poet Nash?'

'No, sir. The poet Herrick.'

'Pretty bitter.'

'Yes, sir.'

'I wonder what they had done to him to stir him up like that. Probably fined him five quid for failing to abate a smoky chimney.'

'As to that I have no information, sir.'

Seated in the old sports model some minutes later and driving to keep my tryst with E. Jimpson Murgatroyd, I was feeling singularly light-hearted for a man with spots on his chest. It was a beautiful morning, and it wouldn't have taken much to make me sing Tra-la as I bowled along. Then I came abaft of the protest march and found myself becalmed. I leaned back and sat observing the proceedings with a kindly eye.

CHAPTER TWO

Whatever these bimbos were protesting about, it was obviously something they were taking to heart rather. By the time I had got into their midst not a few of them had decided that animal cries were insufficient to meet the case and were saying it with bottles and brickbats, and the police who were present in considerable numbers seemed not to be liking it much. It must be rotten being a policeman on these occasions. Anyone who has got a bottle can throw it at you, but if you throw it back, the yell of police brutality goes up and there are editorials in the papers next day.

But the mildest cop can stand only so much, and it seemed to me, for I am pretty shrewd in these matters, that in about another shake of a duck's tail hell's foundations would be starting to quiver. I hoped nobody would scratch my paint.

Leading the procession, I saw with surprise, was a girl I knew. In fact, I had once asked her to marry me. Her name was Vanessa Cook, and I had met her at a cocktail party, and such was her radiant beauty that it was only a couple of minutes after I had brought her a martini and one of those little sausages on sticks that I was saying to myself, 'Bertram, this is a good thing. Push it along.' And in due season I suggested a merger. But apparently I was not the type, and no business resulted.

This naturally jarred the Wooster soul a good deal at the moment, but reviewing the dead past now I could see that my guardian angel had been on the job all right and had known what was good for me. I mean, radiant beauty is all very well, but it isn't everything. What sort of a married life would I have had with the little woman perpetually going on protest marches and expecting me to be at her side throwing bottles at the constabulary? It made me shudder to think what I might have let myself in for if I had been a shade more fascinating. Taught me a lesson, that did – viz. never to lose faith in your guardian angel, because these guardian angels are no fools.

JEW BLUES

What do you do
When you're white and you're blue
Tumbling and spiralling on to the floor?
It's just bad news.

You can lie there all night
But you ain't got de right
To sing de blues.
It ain't for Jews.

We wanna be good, We wanna be loving,
But nobody's pushing and nobody's shoving.
The show hasn't shown up, the business is Biz
So here I am Whoever that is.
Stand back, look out.

A bunch of great friends gathered around, like Ian McShane, Ian La Frenais and Dick Clement. Ian and Dick had their own offices and offered me a space to write and I jumped at it. I was surrounded by great English writers and hadn't had to go to London. We had met years before when they were starting up and I might have helped them along a bit when I was becoming a name as a writer. The film came and went very fast but I was offered a telly series in London called *Mog*, which Ian and Dick were writing, and our mutual friend Allan McKeown was producing, about a burglar who was living in a loony bin to avoid the coppers. It sounded perfect and wouldn't happen for a while so I had time to do Graham's film and even plan *Waiting for Godot*. I was back in action after a terrible fall.

I went to see Woody Allen's *Stardust Memories* by myself and was filled with hope and new enthusiasm. It was by far his best film and stirred some profound emotions in me. What was I doing directing big-budget films? I am a writer who acts: I should be more realistic and say no when such things are offered. I think I could direct telly and make a great job of it, but labouring for years on the same project is not for this soldier!

Living in Los Angeles is a dream come true. As a kid in Canning Town I would daydream about living somewhere the

Me with Lee Lacey

sun shines a lot. It turned out to be better than I'd dreamed. I have great friends and can move around nicely and see a film or watch baseball under blue skies – nothing but blue skies from now on. As a baseball player said to me recently, 'Mart, you got the lady, the flash wheels and people all love you so don't go changing!'

I was also asked by a lady on the street how I could stoop so low as to do an interview for a pornographic magazine (*Penthouse*), with naked women in it. I replied that I love naked women. I see one in my house every day and she likes it well enough too.

The rest of America is far removed from Hollywood and perhaps that is why we co-exist.

We will always need entertainment in times of crisis. I have no doubt that the newly elected president will lead us into dodgy waters and the need for relief will be stronger than ever: people will always need to laugh. I need to be funnier on screen and off. I am a depressive and have come to terms with it, but the majority of this big old world has it a lot worse than me.

In the past few months we have lost our heroes John Lennon and Peter Sellers, which is beyond unbelievable. Ronald Reagan was shot, which was no surprise considering his policies. I am hoping that this will curb his radical beliefs and America will be safe.

I liken my career to that of Simon Rodia, a local hero in Watts, Los Angeles. He built towers out of found materials, mostly junk. He came to Los Angeles from Italy with little or nothing and asked for nothing, but kids and adults enjoy his legacy, which costs them nothing.

They walk among his crazy towers and wonder what they're all about. I feel that I will get there with my work: maybe some kids will poke around, wonder what it's all about, watch me with their mums and dads and giggle.

No reason for reason, no cause for effect,
No time for no season, no course to select.
No way I can stay, I'm leaving because
There went something Whatever that was.
Stand out, look back.

As Mrs Grossfarb reminded me over the counter at Art's Deli recently, 'Your movie was OK. It didn't make me laugh but it made me think and that doesn't happen at the movies too much for me.' She also told me I should work with Barbra Streisand because she is a lovely lady!

Tangier was the primary word I had jammed in my head. We'd had an offer from a pal to stay there for a month, and it couldn't come fast enough. I did a quick turn in a film with Jerry Lewis, which was fun, and I was paid a ridiculous fee, too. My back had really become a burden and I was seeing a doctor in Beverly Hills almost every day. It was becoming obvious that I would have to have surgery. It turns out that, as well as the fused vertebrae, I had damaged my coccyx severely.

I was invited to speak at an anti-handgun event along with Elliott Gould in Washington and said I would. Oh, Tangier, ever closer! I had jumped onboard with the handgun people after John Lennon's death, but I feel efforts to thwart the National Rifle Association through this kind of event is futile.

I was also asked to present an award at the event or maybe introduce the chaps from Second City, the famous comedy club. I wanted to support them, and the likes of *Saturday Night Live* and *SCTV*. Those shows were the only hope for comedy in commercial telly, especially when it came to absurdist writing or political satire. So speaking at their do was fun. Maybe I could rattle them all up a bit.

Me and Elliot Gould

MY SPEECH

I'm glad you could be here tonight, otherwise I'd feel such a bloody fool standing up here talking to an empty room. I'm also glad that I could be here tonight, otherwise you'd feel damn stupid laughing at nothing. I don't know why I'm here tonight – there seems to be some misunderstanding. Somebody called me up and said, 'Don't talk about politics... This show isn't about politics.' Well, of course it is. If you have an attitude towards fundamental beliefs, we loosely call that a philosophy. As soon as you try to apply that philosophy you are into politics, mate, whether you like it or not. Not me, politics from the Greek meaning 'of the citizen'. I'm not a citizen, so that lets me out. I'm an alien. I'm one of those people you advertised for on the Statue of Liberty. Send me your huddled masses, etc., etc., yearning to be free. Well, I answered your ad. I'm your actual huddled mass, and I yearn, and half of what I yearn I pay to the IRS and so I'm entitled to some say in how it's spent. Your country was formed on the admirable principle of no taxation without representation and so, if the IRS will refund every penny of my back taxes, I'll gladly shut up and never be heard from again.

Oddly, as an alien I have certain inalienable rights. I may not vote but I can bitch, kvetch, cavil and otherwise make a nuisance of myself. I have a Green Card, which proves that I exist. In fact only last week the Supreme Court officially decided that aliens are human beings. I'm an official human being. I've been going around being human for the last forty-seven years but I have done it sneakily, hoping that nobody would find out. Now the Supreme Court has let me out of the closet. Isn't it odd? God made me in his own image – you didn't know he looked this weird, did you?

He made me on the morning of the sixth day, a Saturday. He must have had a rough Friday night! Anyway, I was shaving God's face this morning and wondering what I was going to say tonight, because I'm not talking any old rubbish that just came into my head. This is carefully written rubbish and I just decided not to talk about politics. What right does an English comedian living in southern California have to meddle in American politics?

You'd never listen to anyone like that, anyone like Bob Hope. You don't want foreigners telling you how to run your country. People like Henry Kissinger.

In the past, I've tried. When I first came here back in the sixties, I told you what to do and you didn't do it. I said, 'Recognise Red China.' I didn't say it to anybody in particular. I shouted it on the deck of the *Queen Mary* as we came into New York. I think I was drunk. 'Recognise Red China,' I shouted. 'You don't have to invite it over to dinner, just recognise it!'

Ah, there you are, Red China. I didn't recognise you for a minute, standing behind Mao Tse-tung. No, you don't need my advice. This poor little waif should just be grateful to have been taken in. Although I haven't been totally taken in. I wasn't taken in by Mr Reagan or Mr Haig, parenthetically the quick and the dead. Not that I wish to criticise General Haig, and I'm using the word 'general' in the sense we frequently use it, meaning unspecific, undefined, vague as in Haig. May I quote the secretary of state? 'The conduct of international affairs is essentially dialectic, and you have a sine curve of attitudes. We felt there had to be some clearing of the air.' How the hell can you criticise a word of that? How the hell can you understand it?

Mr Haig's pronouncements have been described as Kafkaesque, but Haig suffers from a severe disadvantage in the comparison. Kafka can be translated into English. I don't know what he's talking about. It's rather like *The Emperor's New Clothes*. Not so much that I've noticed he's walking around stark naked, but as a taxpayer, I object to paying the tailor's bill. I mustn't talk about politics! Although I don't really disagree with Mr Haig: he believes that the meek shall inherit the earth after the strong have finished with it, by which time it won't be worth having. But that's my personal opinion and naturally it's subjective. To a fish, Hell is up.

I don't want to seem ungrateful – after all, you sent me food parcels during the war. I still have a half-eaten orange somewhere. America loaned England a lot of money under the Marshall Aid scheme. Allowing for inflation, that works out at $2.35 per person and I brought the money with me tonight in cash. You don't have to put it through the books, so if you can tell me who to give it to . . . I'd like to start out with a clean slate.

You see, I was thinking of applying for American citizenship. I have the form here. I thought I would just come and check out

Washington before I took the leap. It's number nineteen. That bothers me. Nineteen B, to be exact. There might be a problem here. 'Have you ever knowingly sided or supported the Communist Party directly, or indirectly through another organisation, group or person?' Well, I have. I may as well admit it since you're bound to find out anyway. I gave sixpence to Mrs Roosevelt's Aid to Russia fund. There, I've told you, and I'm glad, I tell you, glad. So, you see, in a sense, I'm a fellow traveller although you can't go very far on sixpence.

In the few moments remaining before I'm deported, I ought to get on and perform the function for which I'm here. You see, I'm not just decorative, I'm functional and I'm here tonight to introduce the next item on our grisly little farrago, the Second City Troupe of Strolling Satirists. Satire is not an entirely straight trade and I often suspect the people who ply it of downright happiness, frequently under the guise of being cool, aloof observers of our social mores. I think they're secretly having a bloody good time. They would hate you to know it.

My worst suspicions were confirmed when I watched Second City, for not only do they enjoy themselves, but they're funny too.

Would you please rise? You see, I promised them a standing ovation, so please stand and ovate Second City, or stay where you are and applaud notwithstanding. The Second City people are a great bunch, and a few told me they loved my last film. In the audience there were a lot of older people and I had old ladies telling me that they liked my speech, though they didn't understand my accent but loved me with the puppets!

Change can be slow!
Both Elliott Gould and I were asked to do all sorts of silly things at the show. We were both exhausted: it was July, the heat

was oppressive and our will was waning, to say the least. I was told to keep it short, then go around the crowd and raise more cash. I did so with a bottle of bourbon as my support!

My film came and went, and most people talked about my *Muppet* episode, which is fine: I'm supposed to make people laugh or at least try to.

In 1973 I'd another run of live shows. Now I'm thinking the time for live shows is here again. What with Reagan and Thatcher, the inspiration is there. In the absence of a king, those two would inspire any number of jesters.

I had talked to the great jazz drummer Billy Cobham, whom I had seen play with Miles Davis, my old doppelganger, and decided we should do a jazz-meets-comedy show together in Switzerland where he lives. I'm so excited because I think this may set the groundwork for *Atlantic Crossing*, my planned stage show. Going there in January seems a good way to start the year. I have been secretly planning, with my friend and architect Ted Levy, to design an apartment and hopefully a somewhat plush one in Hampstead that we can own and use when we visit for work or to see friends. Hotels get old fast, and the thought of having a home away from home sounds good. Maybe *Mog* will happen and the apartment will pay off in terms of time spent there.

I can't imagine growing old and being of retirement age, but I know if it happens I'll most likely be in our Los Angeles home, looking forward to the Dodgers getting ready for spring training. I have become quite the fan. As in my Chelsea days, I follow the team that is close to home and enjoy going to the game and having a veggie dog with whoever will accompany me.

OH, LORD

Jesus cured, cared.
The son shone on the holy sea.
He was the word,
First, and last word.
Sent word for His sake forsaken
Across cross, criss cross,
I here time wish you were wonderful

Having been through an intensive period of introspection and self-reassessment I have come to face certain facts about myself. I know that it is the famousness of being famous that I really enjoy and, as a result, acting is my prime source of satisfaction, if only as a means of self-advertisement. This in itself is not ignoble, merely adolescent. The fear of anonymity and death has been my urgency. Immature, yes, but I have to embrace it and make it work for me. I can't run from death, but chase life furiously.

So it seems I must consider myself an actor first. Whether I'm running around in a forest with Mel Brooks or being a pirate in *Yellowbeard* with my chums in Mexico, I must act and regularly, either on telly, the big screen or embarrassing myself on a theatre stage.

Telly is my most immediate lure because it was where I started and had my best success. Maybe it's Mog the burglar: I might convince them to shoot it here and not in the cold and damp of old Blighty.

Writing may come second, but it's something I know I do well.

The inner me and the outer wife both think that is who the real me be.

There are things that one could have prevented in one's life. For me, it might have been a lot easier to stay at home and at school, to eat meat and say 'sure' instead of 'fuck off', to follow in my dad's footsteps and work in his cosy confines. I could have told Lauretta funny jokes, played my trumpet for her and written poems that only she would ever see.

But my mind is an attic full of crazy dreams that never quit or disappoint me, and I have been blessed with these eyEs to see things differently and have people see me in a different way.

I am lucky to have had my family and my brothers: Barry, Spike, Graham, John, Tim, Eric, Chris, Don, Gene, Mel, Peter, on and on, and then the girls that tickle me so, Cissy and Aimi and Teri and Madeline, on and on again.

Surely it was not through luck but intent that I met Lauretta Eleanor Sullivan in a dingy club. That was when the light came on and it continues to shine.

I am a lucky old son.

WANKER PRODUCTIONS
1600 North Highland Avenue ● Hollywood, California 90028
(213) 467-2019

Mr. Steve Garvey
LOS ANGELES DODGERS
1000 Elysian Park Avenue
Los Angeles, CA   90012

Dear Big Steve:

Thank you for your invitation to participate in your
Celebrity Tennis-Racquetball Classic. Unfortunately,
I cannot play tennis. I cannot play racquetball. All
I can play is celebrity.

If I can be of any non-playing assistance, then time
permitting I'd be delighted to help, what is obviously
a very worthy cause. If anything occurs to you, please
feel free to call, write, send carrier pigeon, smoke
signals or convey messages with jungle drums.

I remain yours, but I have no idea in what capacity,

                              Marty Feldman

I have some great film ideas and have been writing furiously in a nice office close to Hollywood Boulevard, with writers all around me. It reminds me of my many years with Barry, though not as exciting. I just got a letter from Barry, which said:

LETTER FROM BARRY TOOK

I remember, frequently and fondly, days, nights and weeks we spent hammering out everything we could think of for anyone who would use it. Perhaps it's like remembering past holidays, when you only recall the sunny days. I know it rained during our eight-year holiday – by George, it pissed down, didn't it? But overall it was good, wasn't it? We didn't know what we couldn't do, so we did every damn thing, and I tittered and bit my nails, and your ears hurt from laughing and it was fucking fine work, laddie. Oh, what larks, Pip!

Now there you are and here I am, or the other way around, and it will never be the same again or maybe it will. I'd like to think it will.

My love to you and yours, stay well and write soon.

I pinch your claw,

P. T. Gruntfuttock (Upholsterer to the Gentry since 1847)

This great man makes me forget all my quibbles with myself and my country, and makes me want to jump on a plane and pinch his claw too. Perhaps I will and would love it because there is magic there and it never goes away. With time spent for bad behaviour, it seems like a bloody good idea.

I know that as writer I can't do it alone, if not with Barry or Chris or Graham or Peter Cook. It's probable that I'm not suited to the long form. Sketches are what I write best. The sketch to the play stands as the short story to the novel. I am not Balzac but only Guy de Maupassant and that is nothing to be ashamed of. The sketch form lends itself best to the kind of anarchic comedy I do best.

So a movie is not a thing I want to make primary in my concerns. I have offers from Europe through a new company called Polygram, based here. It could only be of interest if it was a series of sketches. That is basically what *Python* is all about, sketch in film form and bloody good too.

I conclude that, given the above and accepting that, although the offers are there, I must temporarily retreat to what is working for now, as I grow a beard for the first time in my life, at the brave age of forty-eight!

I will take up the position that what I do I must do best. As Gene and Mel lead the way for me in films here, I must serve you all and happily play the clown, which, increasingly, it appears is where I belong.

With Harry and my very first beard!

I will always be a Marxist/anarchist or, as they say now, eclectic. That is where the clown dwells best, but with heart, for that alone should lead us.

I have always had a love-hate relationship with words because they are mostly ambitious. That is why I became a physical performer. Vocally, I am limited: I have a soft voice, which doesn't penetrate, and have fought with great difficulty to overcome a lisp, which I developed at an early age and still hear squeaking in here and there.

I didn't come into this profession just to make money. I have always loved writing comedy and I am lucky to get paid for it but I would do it if I weren't, and happily so.

Acting is just a bonus. Living is the fun part, which I am learning to do better with my love and guiding light, Lauretta.

Off for now to play I must. Much love, my darlings . . . Please stay tuned or, at the very least, stay!

Tangier at last!

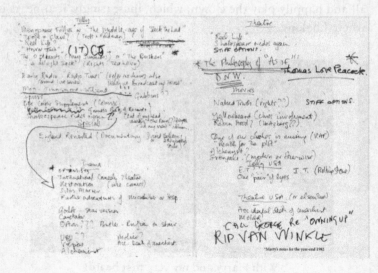

For Lauretta
Because I love
you.

Marty

LONG LIVE THE CLOWN

Satire is not an entirely straight trade. I'm often suspicious of people who practise this crooked craft of happiness. They'd hate it to be known, of course, but it is our duty to let them run free. Some of them have broken their backs in the attempt to make us laugh. Rave on, you happy/miserable professionals!

END

Lauretta lay on the Spanish tiles of their kitchen floor and wouldn't get up when she heard that Marty was gone. She said she wanted to die. Her friends filled her house every day and night but she wanted to be alone. She said that all she could think was, What am I going to do now when I get bad news? She told the story many times of standing in her kitchen, crying, having just received a phone call from London and learning that her elder brother had died. Marty had walked through the back door, home early from work. He saw her crying and, without asking, held and hugged her. He told her to cry and let it all out. When she finally calmed down a little she said, 'My brother has just died.'

Marty said, 'So I suppose now is not the time to tell you I'm leaving you!'

He always found a way.

A funeral was arranged. Marty was to be buried next to his hero Buster Keaton, a coveted location at Forest Lawn cemetery. She knew that he would have preferred to be cremated but didn't challenge any decision that was made. She said he used to joke that he wished to be cremated and have his friends snort his ashes.

Her friends tried to get her out of the house but she said she felt safer there because the house was home and very much both of them. She said that Marty would constantly say he was pinching himself to make sure the happiness he felt in their home was real.

She felt numb by it all. She didn't want to go to the funeral, even though all of their friends would be there. Those who couldn't make it sent kind words. She said, 'It was a Kafkaesque nightmare.'

A month later, when Graham Chapman returned from completing his film *Yellowbeard*, he asked if he could drop by. Lauretta was packing her bags for a trip to Australia to get away from it all. They sat together and drank tea outside. Graham told her that the autopsy showed Marty's arteries had been blocked.

She had known it, and they agreed that Marty had too. He never had shut up about dying young. She remembered them sitting by the pool at the hotel in Mexico on the day she was leaving, shortly before Marty died. He was speaking to a journalist about death. She had asked him to change the subject and eventually got angry with him. She was getting on a plane soon and didn't want to hear him talking about his death. They never said goodbye, a habit they had formed at their first meeting. It was either 'See you at the thing' or 'Very well, then' but never 'Goodbye'. They joked that Graham might have been partly responsible for starting Marty's acting career but hadn't thought he would also be responsible in some way for its end.

Lauretta remembered Graham's kindness and warmth: she said that talking to him and his son, John, helped take a little of the pain away.

She had been angry with Marty for leaving her. Graham told her that Marty's last words were sweet and funny. He had said things that only Marty would say. He had told Graham to tell her, 'I love you very much and I am so happy I never had to put my thing in anyone else.'

Marty had shot a scene on his final day and spent the afternoon running around the markets and shops looking for little presents for his old lady. He showed Graham's son John all that he had bought. He complained about his aching back and his chronic constipation but was full of life and looking forward to going home. He couldn't wait to get back to work and said his head was exploding with ideas. John said that Marty had hugged him and retreated to his room.

John Boorman, the great English director, wrote to Lauretta shortly after Marty's death. He told her that he and his wife Christel had bumped into Marty on the Sunday before he had died and they'd had drinks together, joined by the actor Michael Hordern. They had been impressed with how slim and relaxed Marty looked, and said that he was in great form. He was complaining of severe pain at the base of his spine but was otherwise happy. He also said he couldn't wait to get home, that Lauretta had left that morning to take care of 'the nuts and bolts'. In the letter John said he had met Marty many times and felt that they had grown up together. Of an age, they had shared a common time and place. John had witnessed Marty's whole career from the radio writing onwards, and said he felt indebted to Marty for countless laughs and years of pleasure.

Marty had opted not to join them that evening for dinner but he walked a few blocks towards the restaurant with them. Finally he turned his back, his hands clasped behind him, and, with a kind of comic dignity, he disappeared into the milling masses. John said that it had been a warm and pleasant interlude with a man at the height of his powers. They couldn't believe he was gone and said that 'Sorrow and grief are lonely to bear', and they shared her loss.

That letter meant so much to Lauretta. She didn't read many of the hundreds she received until some years after his death.

LETTER FROM SPIKE

14 December 1982

My dear Lauretta,

As you know words are bloody useless at a time like this, but you know how I feel.

When you come over, please see me.

It was a terrible loss for me, God knows how much it was a loss for you. He wasn't just a funny man, he was a bloody nice fellow.

If life is a game of cards, somebody is cheating.

Love Spike

A NOTE FOUND ON A NAPKIN IN MARTY'S POCKET AFTER HE DIED

The function of my comedy is not to provide answers, but to postulate questions, impertinent questions and therefore, finally, pertinent questions. Not to open doors, merely to unlock them. Not to invade the boundaries of probability but stand a cool guard this side of the boundaries. Somewhere between there's a thesis. To pump up the muscle of dialectic (or in my case Di-Eclectic!) against the brawn of surrealistic solution.

I play not Hamlet, but the second gravedigger, not Lear but the fool.

CREDITS

Produced and edited by Mark Flanagan.

Photographic editing and design by Lincoln DeFer. Editing assistance from Tom Brosseau.

Special thanks to . . .

Lauretta and Renee, Mahalia, Seamus, Jon and Paul (Dos Amigos), Anne Levy, Stan, Julian, Don, Van Dyke, Anthony, Marie, Jenny McNeill-Galle, Maya, Pearl, Lucy, Jack, Betsy, Scott, Ellen, Guillermo, Michael Griffee, Weston and all the Dixons, Dave 'Gruber' Allen, Paul F. Tompkins, Greg Proops, and everybody at Largo (old and new) who knew and loved Lauretta.

Very special thanks to Eric Idle for being so supportive and a gentleman, and everything that you would hope he would be.

I would like to thank Mark Booth and Fiona Rose at Coronet for making this story, which was found in a box, in an attic after being alone for 30 years, available to all.

For all things Marty check out www.theofficialmartyfeldman.com

PHOTOGRAPHIC ACKNOWLEDGEMENTS

Edwin Sampson / Associated Newspapers /REX Shutterstock, Evening Standard/Getty Images, Ben Jones/REX Shutterstock, Trinity Mirror/Mirrorpix/Alamy Stock Photo, JON LYONS/REX Shutterstock, Bettmann/CORBIS, NBC/NBCU Photo Bank via Getty Images, Eric Hands, BBC Photo Library, Bettmann/CORBIS, Terry O'Neill/Getty Images, Michael Ochs Archives/Universal/Getty Images, Courtesy Everett Collection, Universal/courtesy Everett Collection, David Dagley/REX Shutterstock, Photos 12/Alamy Stock Photo.

All other photographs are from private collections.

Thanks for reading Marty's story.

The proceeds from this adventure will go to: the Flanman Children's Tumor Fund, a foundation that will distribute financial support to any organisations working on a cure for or the treatment and care of children with tumours.

Mark Flanagan, Trustee of The Marty Feldman Estate and loving friend of Lauretta Eleanor Feldman, with all her raging beauty

My looks are my equipment, my comic equipment, and they are the right packaging for my job. Not the right packaging for a brain surgeon or the pilot of a 747, but I have the right packaging for a clown. I need comedy and there's nothing degrading about playing the fool.